THE
GIRL
WHO
FELL TO
EARTH

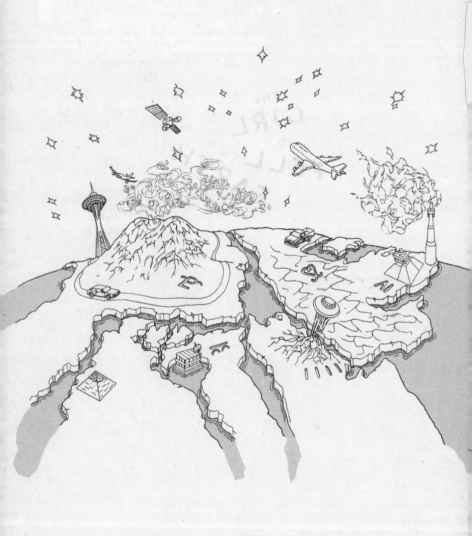

HARPER ● PERENNIAL

NEW YORK • LONDON • TORONTO • SYDNEY • NEW DELHI • AUCKLAND

THE
GIRL
WHO
FELL TO
EARTH

A MEMOIR BY

SOPHIA
AL-MARIA

HARPER PERENNIAL

THE GIRL WHO FELL TO EARTH. Copyright © 2012 by Sophia Al-Maria. All rights reserved. Printed in the United States of America. No part of this book may be used or reproduced in any manner whatsoever without written permission except in the case of brief quotations embodied in critical articles and reviews. For information, address HarperCollins Publishers, 195 Broadway, New York, NY 10007.

HarperCollins books may be purchased for educational, business, or sales promotional use. For information, please e-mail the Special Markets Department at SPsales@harpercollins.com.

Map on page ii by Chris Kwung.

FIRST EDITION

Designed by Fritz Metsch

Library of Congress Cataloging-in-Publication Data is available upon request.

ISBN 978-0-06-199975-8

16 17 18 19 20 OV/RRD 10 9 8 7 6 5 4 3 2

Greetings!
May time bring us together.

تحياتنا للأصدقاء في النجوم.
يا ليت يجمعنا الزمان.

—Arabic recording on the Voyager Spacecraft Golden Records

CONTENTS

THE GIRL WHO FELL TO EARTH

PROLOGUE
OH EYE, OH NIGHT

This story begins with a winking star. Dusk is falling across the Arabian Gulf and with it comes Maghreb prayer. Only after the sun has set and the shoulder-angels have been greeted will the stars come out on the television. The year is 1969, and the Lebanese songbird Samira Tawfik prepares to perform live from a studio at Kuwait TV. "Look to him," the director orders, gesturing to the cameraman. "Right there into his lens." Samira obliges, raising her veil and fanning her lashes slowly at the big, black pupil of the camera. The director scurries back into the control room to survey the effect from an ellipse of black-and-white monitors. He smiles. The illusion is working! Samira's faces are shining down on him like a dozen silvery moons, and just like a fixed star or a portrait painting, no matter where he moves she seems to be looking at only him. In a few minutes on televisions all across the Arabian Peninsula, Samira will appear to look, with loving attention, into the eyes of each viewer.

The orchestra sits politely across from the singer, arrayed on a bandstand painted to look like a cosmic keyboard stretching infinitely into the backdrop. Even standing on her raised plinth, Samira's sequined gown columns clear to the floor. Her hair is both beehived and braided for the appearance, a clever combination evoking Bedouin girl and modern city lady at the same time.

"You gazelle! Ya Samira! Somewhere out there is a boy who'll have his heart broken tonight," the director jokes through the talkback loudspeaker. The orchestra chortles, the cameraman nods his approval. It's true.

The metal microphone juts at attention under Samira's chin, straining up to catch the sound of her breath as she holds it in wait for the distant athan to finish. "I can't sing a love song without at least one broken heart," she mews, shrugging with coquettish indifference.

The call-to-prayer falls silent and the countdown-to-live begins. The TV cameras wheel through their orbit into position. Samira closes her eyes and whispers just before her cue, "Ya ain, ya layl"—"Oh Eye, Oh Night"—and the airways open to her song.

1

LAMBDA LEONIS • THE GLANCE •
الطرف

Eighty miles out of Al-Hasa oasis in the Eastern Province of Saudi Arabia, a Bedouin boy named Matar was flicking the knob of a portable General Electric television on and off. He was waiting with a crowd of other kids for Maghreb prayer, when the sun would set and the imam would finally turn the generator on. Only then could their night begin and with it, the TV! Or *al-tel-ay-veez-yawn*, as they affectionately called it. Like the watering well, the long-drop outhouse, and everything else in the tiny settlement of Kuzahmiah, the TV was for communal use. But unlike the other shared utilities of the town, it commanded pride of place in the courtyard of their one-room mosque, much to the disappointment of the devout young imam. The imam had moved from the big city to the Bedouin settlement hoping to find a *pure* Islam, untainted by modernity. But the spiritual authenticity he sought from the members of the Al-Dafira tribe was a fantasy made most obvious to him by their love of the TV. Attached by wires to an antenna of steel ribbons artfully bent into the rough onion-shaped spire, the town's boys had strung the latticework of jury-rigged wires up alongside the

minaret on the mud roof of the little mosque. This vexed
the imam, who often complained to the patriarchs of the
tribe at Friday prayer about this. "Your television tower is
taller than the minaret! Do you think this is acceptable?"
But no one seemed to care about these details as long as they
didn't miss an episode of *Lost in Space*. "Your children are
being tempted away right under your noses," he warned. But
the practical people of Al-Dafira were unbothered with the
symbolic blasphemy the imam saw in a few inches of wire.

Every night an illuminated title-card of Quran shone coldly from the screen, silencing the children, who were trans-
fixed in wait for the moment they'd be treated to a song or a
cartoon. On this particular night, it was the beaming face of
Samira Tawfiq that appeared to them. Her voice was beck-
oning and plaintive as she began with a modest *mawwāl*:
"AaaaA-AaaaA." Her wordless melody peaked across the
airwaves and the crowd of barefoot children in the oil-field
wasteland scrambled to get closer. A little boy named Matar
watched. And his heart soared, then dropped, in unison
with the warbling voice as Samira sang, with a cheeky grin,
of returning to an abandoned abode. "Yesterday afternoon I
went by where he lives. But I found nothing. Only sadness."

Matar noticed the deep dimple in her cheek when she
smiled and wondered why she was so happy when this was
supposed to be a sad song. But his critical thinking was
halted when something new happened: Samira looked directly into the camera—directly at Matar. He froze in her
headlights; she winked! The string section swept upward to
take the reins of the song, and the little boy went supernova
with delight.

"She saw me! She winked at me! She loves me!"

He was jumping mid-crow when his older brother Mohamed cuffed him flat. "She was winking at *me*, retard," he growled.

Mohamed then trapped Matar easily in a sunset flip, shoulders pinned by knees until Matar fell limp. He knew his bear of a brother would lose interest if he played dead—he just hoped it happened before Samira's song was over.

It was around this time that the ten-year-old Matar began keeping a diarized account of his life in an old book of graph paper. He took detailed notes in blue pencil of his quotidian: what time he woke, how many times he prayed, how far they traveled—how long that took, how many times his brother Mohamed picked a fight, and columns to track who won. Matar wrote all about what he ate and how it tasted; what he watched on TV and how it rated. It was as though he were afraid of leaving anything behind—and that was strange for a Bedouin boy.

The following is the sequence of programming on Dhahran TV as remembered by Matar. The schedule, from what he understood, was calibrated by the Saudi Aramco Oil Company. At the time he was moved into the Kuzahmiah settlement, it ran something like this:

18:00—*Looney Tunes* or *Popeye*. Olive Oyl was translated into Arabic as *Zeitoonah*, and this is what Matar nicknamed his lanky, cow-hocked older sister Moody.

18:30—Children's hour: *Mr. Ed, Lassie,* or both. A few years later came *Little House on the Prairie*, which was a runaway hit. The settling traumas of the Ingalls girls struck

5

a chord with Bedu kids being relocated to villages like Kuzahmiah from scattered camps that had been caught in the drill lights of oil derricks.

19:30—News, with auspicious tidings of the king's good health as the lead item; once Matar remembers seeing American astronauts bouncing on the moon.

20:00—*Asha* prayer, more Quran.

20:15—*Perry Mason*, *Rawhide*, or *Star Trek*. Being the town Trekkie, Matar kept particularly detailed anthropological notes of the alien tribes and cultures in the show.

21:30—An Egyptian comedy, an Indian musical, or an American western.

But the imam usually cut the generator early, whether or not the film had ended. Even though the imam was an intelligent and educated young man, he was also deeply suspicious of the television broadcasts. Were they *meant* to make Al-Dafira children prize the deserts of America over their own? The crowd of kids would groan in such bitter disappointment when the cowboys lost. And he resented that the children had to watch Robert Mitchum stride into a saloon, gulp a shot of whiskey, and then growl in classical Arabic: "Hey, partner, thanks for the cold tea, I needed it." The broadcast would fizzle into static with cool finality and the imam would break the gathering of sleepy kids, wading through the pool of boys and girls, long braids spread over bare feet, and send them home. The older kids usually took his cue out of respect and slung their younger siblings onto their hips to leave. But while they scattered into the dark doorways of their homes to dream of cowboys and border collies, Matar remained stubbornly in front of the TV fantasizing about space travel. He furiously noted all the action down in blue graphite. It was only when he caught a glimpse of the imam's reflection smoldering from the darkened screen that Matar would rise and shuffle reluctantly along the treads of the one truck in town to his home. As he stumbled along the dark path strewn with goat turds, he often saw, through bleary eyes, a faceless figure float toward him. It would bounce in the dust, as weightless as a man on the moon. This *khayal*, or shadow, followed him, keeping watch from behind its mirrored visor, a mask that reflected a bowed version of Matar's world back to him, letting him see things he couldn't alone. But the *khayal* always disappeared when he reached the standard-issue government hut where his family slept. Then Matar would crawl into his bed of wool blankets and jumbled siblings and stare up through a crack in the ceiling *just* wide enough for him to make out a few weak stars.

Matar was old enough to remember a time before his clan had gotten situated into settled life. Back then, their nights were longer. He had spent very little time with his father, Jabir, who was a wilderness detective for the police and had become famous for his tracking abilities. Able to tell if a missing woman was pregnant by her footprints and to intuit the moves of a criminal on the run "like a hawk to a snake in the open," Jabir was the last of his kind. Matar *had* managed to pick up some practical desert skills from his father—which cracks in the sand might bare truffles, as well as more uncanny skills, like how to tell a storm was coming by the patterns in the sand. But all matters to do with the sky he learned from his mother, Safya.

Safya had married Jabir when she was fourteen. Like everyone back then, Safya and Jabir were cousins. He had taken her from a tough family of the larger Dafira tribe who kept within the borders of the Empty Quarter, an infamous desert where the night sky was laden heaviest with the Milky Way.

When Matar was little, they still kept far from Doha or Al-Hasa, where the city light smeared an electric haze on the atmosphere. After long days of travel, Safya bunted her hungry children and talked them to sleep, teaching her first three children, Mohamed, Moody, and Matar, the names and shapes of all the stars and constellations she knew. Curled at her sides, shielded from the wind by the saddle-matted hump of their mother's camel, they'd repeat as she pointed:

"Al-Firq."

"The Flock."

"Al-Anka."

"The Phoenix."

And "Al-Difdi."

"The Frog."

When they came to an antiquated or explicit name like Al-Maraqq (the Genitalia), she would say "that bit between the belly and the legs," translating the meanings she knew for them and wondering to herself about those she didn't. It was an effective pacifier for the long nights in the deep desert. But even when folded under their blanket of sky, Matar was often unable to sleep for the wattage of the stars.

Then one night when Matar was sick with fever, Safya stroked his sweaty forehead and distracted him from the chills: "Choose a star and it's yours."

Matar squinted up from his misery at all the twinkling possibilities. They were extra vivid from the fever, changing from silver to pale pink and back again. He felt rich and spoiled for choice at all these shimmers in the sky, appearing like the shiny pieces of metal his mother sewed onto her woolly black winter cloak. Head cradled in his mother's lap, Matar settled on the westernmost of the two stars known as the First Leap. She smiled because he had chosen west, the direction of Mecca: "Someday you'll go and I'll be proud of you."

But Safya could never have guessed how far west her son would want to go, or what destiny was manifesting itself for him there.

2

XI URSAE MAJORIS •
THE FIRST LEAP • القفزة الأولى

Over the years, the pale tungsten glow of Al-Hasa continued to spread over the sky to their north, bleeding its uncolored light farther and farther into the desert. The brighter it grew, the more difficult it was to see the stars. Compared with the poverty they were used to on their travels, not having to carry your weight in water was positively luxuriant. But convenience and security had a price, paid largely by Safya and the women of the tribe, who began a long, slow retreat into the concrete domesticity of modern sedentary life. The girls of Al-Dafira, who were used to herding and foraging and riding long distances in the sun, were now napping in the shade. In the desert they wore bright calico dresses and pierced their noses and wore long braids plaited into threes, out in the open without veils. Where they used only to cover their faces they now covered their whole bodies in black, a new custom invented to protect their honor (and identities) now that they lived in closer proximity to neighbors with forked tongues.

Military service emerged as the best option for boys like Matar and Mohamed. With reputations as tough, loyal fighters, Bedouin boys from Al-Dafira were sought after by the Saudi government as well as surrounding emirates. When he turned sixteen, Mohamed enlisted in the air force of the nearby emirate of Qatar. There he was given the benefit of citizenship and was trained to be a jet pilot, eventually racking up enough flying hours to be the first to fly an F-16 Fighting Falcon. When Matar came of age he wanted to distinguish himself from his brother and went in for the navy. However, unlike the majority of his company, who had grown up in villages along the rocky coastline fishing and pearl-diving, Matar couldn't swim. Up until the first week of training he had never even *seen* the sea, let alone been in or on it. He lasted a total of five seasick days before his commander took him aside and said, "Stick to the sand, Bedu boy."

Matar returned home after his dismissal and, feeling humiliated by his failure at sea, resolved to prove everyone wrong by going far beyond where any of the tribe had ever been. He wasn't sure just where that was yet, but he knew it was somewhere else. Then one day as he idled the family's GMC truck in Al-Hasa waiting for his father to finish haggling with a herdsman over a pair of goats, the radio picked up an official announcement that Qatar was giving scholarships for young men to go to "the America." He took down the information and began making a plan. The next week, Matar shaved, bought a clean *thobe* and a pair of aviator mirror-shades, borrowed the GMC, and headed to the big city of Doha.

He spent three days waiting in the limbo of random

corridors at the Ministry of Education, a leaflet for an English school in Seattle, "Home of the Space Needle," folded into his chest pocket. On it was a color photograph of rolling mountains and in the foreground what looked like a giant rocket ship. It reminded him of a hazy boyhood memory of a shadow who used to visit him at night, the silver man, the Astronaut. When his interview came, Matar showed the pamphlet.

The bureaucrat who oversaw scholarships was surprised. "Don't you want to be in a *big* city? New York? Los Angeles? Dearborn? There will be more *Arabs* there. Friends!" the man urged.

But Matar had heard of none of these exotic metropolises. The bureaucrat shook his head and took Matar's papers. "As you like. You Bedu boys are strange." He had a look at the leaflet for Seattle and flipped through it doubtfully. "None of our students have gone there yet. You'll be on your own. Alone. Do you understand?"

Matar nodded, though he didn't really comprehend any of it. He was already rapt in a fantasy of riding a rocket through the snowy mountains, bellying up to a bar and ordering cold tea from a glass bottle with Robert Mitchum.

Within a week, it was all arranged. Matar returned to Kuzahmiah with a briefcase full of his tuition in traveler's checks and a newly minted passport declaring him a Qatari citizen.

"Where are you going?" his mother asked as he sat visiting with her and his sisters inside the hut while they spun camel hair into large spools of frizzy yarn.

He showed them his plane ticket, written by hand in Arabic, bound for "New York, JFK" and continuing on to "Seattle, USA."

"How far is it to drive there?" Safya asked him matter-of-factly.

"Too far," he said. Why mention the thousands of miles of sea and mountains? It would only worry her.

Safya seemed satisfied by that answer, the wise matron who had traveled more miles on foot than most humans ever would in a lifetime, remarkably innocent of how far "far away" could really be.

Matar's first pair of trousers belonged to a dead man. They were not quite what he'd imagined for himself, but Western clothes were hard to come by in the Al-Hasa market. He bought a used polyester suit from a widow whose husband had been fond of going to Cairo's cabarets and mingling with bell-bottomed *shaabi* singers like Ahmed Adawiya. The outfit for his journey west was dusty pink and three pieces: pants, waistcoat, and jacket. Matar pulled off the road on his way back to Kuzahmiah to try them on in private. He headed down the road past the derricks and parked behind a jagged boulder big enough to hide the truck. He didn't want anyone to see him; it was indecent the way his legs would show.

Parked behind the monument, Matar pulled the salmon pink slacks on and wrestled himself into the top. He had been bare-bottomed as a baby and shoeless until he was twelve; now he was eighteen and wearing pants for the first time ever. They were tight, *very tight*, at the crotch, and he was used to the easy breeze of loose cotton *sirwal* under his *thobe*. He imagined this might be what his sisters felt wearing *abayas* for the first time: embarrassed, clumsy, and uncomfortable while figuring out how and where to fold, button, and tuck. Matar angled the side mirror on the GMC up and down to catch small glimpses of the overall effect. Silhouetted against the sunset, he looked pretty good. His hair was long and straight to his shoulders; he had a sleek, black mustache; and his skin was dark and smooth. But even in the dead man's duds he looked nothing like the Americans he'd seen on television.

Matar was illiterate in English, but that was an easy dune to scramble up compared with the mountain of cultural difference he would have to climb. He packed a few pairs of *sirwal* in his briefcase, along with a palm-sized green leather Quran that zipped up on the sides. He didn't make any official good-byes to anyone but his sisters and mother. Bedouin bid farewell casually if at all, a habit from traveling paths so tightly woven that a hello was never far from a good-bye. He kissed the foreheads of all his sisters and then his mother, Safya, who patted at the lapels of his strange clothing and commented disapprovingly on the pink, spongy material: "This looks like a goat tongue." He could see she was worried from the sliver of furrowed brow that showed between her *berga* and her braids.

"I'll be fine," he said as much for his own benefit as hers. "They've sent many others before me," he lied.

Still, even if she could not understand how far into the unknown her son was about to go, she had known from the time he was a child that this moment would come.

They all gathered and waved him off as he climbed into the truck, duded up like a dandy and feeling foolish alongside his father, who sat silent in the driver seat. Matar and his father made their way off-road to the highway leading over the border and to Doha. They pulled up amid the bustle of the airport. Matar stepped out and walked around the truck to his father's open window, where he sat, engine idling alongside the sunken curb, long gray beard ruffling in the exhaust as he squinted through the heat at his son.

"*Estowda'a Allah al lethi la yethia'a wada'ai*," he said, which in English translates roughly to "I entrust my treasure to Allah, the only one who never loses precious things."

And with that, he swung the pickup around and drove off, leaving his son to fly into the sunset, secure in the belief that whatever fate befell him would be Allah's will.

Matar traveled with the edge of night to a point so far and so different from his home it might as well have been another planet. He thought vague, celestial thoughts as he rested his head against the window in the plane. He craned his eyes to the sky and picked out his star, remembering the nights wedged against his mother's breast in the Empty Quarter. The flight was long and uncomfortable, and the dead man's suit pinched him everywhere, exacerbating the situation. He sweated right through it with anxiousness, fretting in his delirium after the tenth hour of darkness that the sun might not rise again. At JFK airport he wandered from gate to gate following arrows, unable to decipher anything but logos and numbers.

Finally he matched the Pan Am logo with his ticket and went to the counter, where the stewardess squinted at his Arabic itinerary and turned to her supervisor. "This one thinks we read Chinese. Oh brother."

"Where. Are. You. Go-ing?" the supervisor asked. Matar grinned at her. He didn't know what to do but be friendly. She waved her hand in front of his face, pointed at the ticket, and asked an exasperated "where?" by putting her palms up to the sky. Matar did his best at reading the transliterated name for her, "See-Tull." The supervisor and the stewardess both listened carefully until something clicked. "Seattle!" Matar almost clapped at the breakthrough.

"Send him on the next flight out to SeaTac. They'll know what to do with him there—just get him out of our hair," said the supervisor. And within an hour he was on his way again.

Matar had never been *truly* lost in his life until he exited the airport in Washington State and found himself in a torrential rainstorm. In the desert he could orient himself by the stars, the sand, and an internal compass so well aligned to magnetic fields he'd never had to use the handheld kind. A cab pulled up, and Matar ducked to the window.

"Hotel? Sleep?" The cabby knew a fresh-off-the-boat when he saw one. He cupped his hands together and closed his eyes in a blissful expression indicating rest. Matar got in.

Once deposited in a budget room in the Ballard Motel, Matar slept for a day. It was dark outside again when he awoke around 1 a.m. Here there were no stars, only dull light reflecting off a low canopy of gray clouds. The landscape could not have been more alien to him. Tacoma's mayor at the time described what had once been known as the City of Destiny as looking "bombed out like downtown Beirut." The smelly old paper mills, the crumbling brickwork of Union Station, the lurkers, the lounge cats—it was a seedy place that had been in decline since the eureka in the Klondike.

Matar was hungry, but he was also afraid to leave. He sat at the window and looked out onto the still road running outside the hotel. A wino weaved in and out of rowed streetlamps. A distant freight train whistled in the misty dark. He turned on the TV and was dimly comforted by *Star Trek* reruns. Dawn finally came, but the sun didn't rise with it. Instead the clouds lit up, changing their color from night to periwinkle blue. Matar was unable to ascertain the direction of the *Kaaba* with clouds obscuring the direction of the sun. He finally guessed a position and laid out a hotel towel in place of a prayer-rug on the ground, hoping he'd be forgiven if he missed his target.

The next afternoon, when Matar woke, he found the phone number for the school in Seattle. Dialing out from the hotel was frustrating. From Tacoma, Seattle was long distance and so required a certain native knowledge of the U.S. telephone service. Aimless and starving, Matar went into the street, determined to figure it out. He stopped at a gas station and bought a bottle of Pepsi and what he thought he recognized as a box of cornflakes, the lettering of which was a close match to cornflakes back home. Pushing his purchases over the counter at the attendant, he hang-tenned his hand into the international symbol for phone. The teenager behind the till pointed out at a booth across the road and doled him out a stack of quarters just as rippling gray sheets of clouds rolled off the Puget Sound and opened a precision shower overhead. Matar bounded out across the road, soaking his polyester, and skidded into the booth. He pulled the folded paper from his wallet and read off the comforting

Arabic numerals, matching them to the American number buttons.

The phone rang three times; a woman picked up. "Seattle Language Center?"

"Hallo!" Matar, overexcited, yelled into the receiver, "I. Am. Matar."

A pause.

"Hallo!"

"Yes, this is the Seattle Language Center."

"I. Am. Study. Inside. In. You . . ." He paused, searching for the right word, while the woman on the other end, used to foreign students, just let that one go.

"Yes, hello? Where are you?"

Matar looked around for a sign. The first one he saw he read out slowly, "I. Am. On. Speed . . ."

"Speed?"

"Limit. Sixty."

"Is this a crank call? I'm sick of you yay-hoos calling here!" Matar tried to piece her sentence out slowly but couldn't decipher it. "Well?!" Matar could gather that her voice was welling up with annoyance but couldn't make any sound come out of his own mouth. "Damn it. Try it again and I'm calling the police!"

Matar winced at the clang of her hanging up. The dial tone seeped into his ear, a blank, featureless plane of sound that caused a mild panic to rise in his chest. He opened the box of cornflakes, expecting a crunchy snack, but all he scooped up was a mealy white-and-blue powder. He read the name on the box: "Tide." Matar went into the quiet paralysis that

comes with the understanding that you are helpless. Lightning raged over the empty street and he reassured himself—
the best way to weather a storm was to wait in one place
until it passed.

Panes of water rippled the windows of the booth and
Matar waited for a path, a hint, a sign. His sign came in blue
neon, a pair of eyes at the end of the block flashing on and
off. The rain was still coming when he made for the buzz-
ing sign, big blue eyes, and white-hot starbursts that sparked
over the words "Bowling Lanes."

3

GAMMA GEMINORUM •
THE SHINING ONE • الميسان

On this particular night at that particular Tacoma bowling alley, a girl named Gale Valo was waiting for her cousin to get off work. She sat smoking cigarettes over a Formica table and flipping through a decade-old *Life* magazine. It was full of cockeyed photographs of the moon's crater under headlines like "The Eagle Has Landed." Gale had just returned home to the Pacific Northwest after a brief stint in New York, where she had gone hoping to find a place in the leggy lineup of Rockettes at Radio City Music Hall, but failed. Gale was staring into the fishbowl of Buzz Aldrin's gold-plated visor and wondering if she'd ever get another chance to get out of this town.

That's when a "good-looking, kind of dark-skinned guy" slid into a seat a few booths down from where she was sitting. He was young and bedraggled, and looked very, *very* lonesome. Gale watched him through the smoke of her cigarette, leaving it to burn down to the butt. He looked frightened, eyes wide but cast down into a box of Tide laundry detergent. Gale recognized the look of shock: it was the stock-still stare of a spooked horse, eyes rolled and very still. She wondered what she could do to calm him. It took Matar a few minutes to notice Gale staring at him. When he finally did, she blushed and raised her whole head to the cigarette for a drag, "like a little goat trying to eat a tall tree," Matar noted.

Someone put "Satellite of Love" on the jukebox over the rumble of balls and pins and waxed pine. The lyrics were simple. Almost simple enough for Matar to grasp the chorus as Gale mouthed it silently to herself, tapping her foot in time on the polished floor. She went back to her magazine while he earnestly studied her from across the room. She wore black clothing he'd never seen before, tight at the hips and low at the bib. Her hair was sandy yellow, like sixteen-karat gold dulled down in the fog of cigarette smoke. She had it folded into two loose plaits, reminding him of his boyhood dream girl, Samira Tawfiq. He concentrated on her mouth as she lip-synched the song. The words from the jukebox were hard to recognize, but when he read them from her lips they were clear, simple, comprehensible. "I *love* to watch things on TV."

Gale felt Matar's eyes on her and kept a thousand-yard stare on her Marlboro. As the song trailed off at the end, she stabbed out her smoke and met the brown boy's gaze straight on.

A hyped-up group of jocks burst into the alley and headed toward the table Gale sat at. Without looking at them, she slid out of the booth and sidled over to the young man with long wet hair and pink bell-bottoms. "Mind if I sit with you?" she asked in a put-on kind of tough. Matar smiled dumbly back up at her. "What's the matter. Are you shy?"

This question flummoxed him.

"Never mind," she said, tossing her copy of *Life* and her soft pack of cigarettes onto the table. Matar was dazzled by this *real* American girl, and he desperately wanted to talk to her. Just sitting down beside him, Gale had put Matar at ease for the first time since he had landed. At the table where Gale had been sitting, the crowd of rowdy guys in numbered shirts was hooting "Happy Birthday."

"Today is . . . birthday, me," he lied.

"Well, then, we'll celebrate!" she announced and trotted to the bar, returning to the table with two squat brown Rainier bottles and sitting back down across from him. Matar hesitated at the bottle. "Oh, crap. Did you want a glass? I'm sorry." Gale went back to the bar for a cold glass. Her posture was one of a hostess, graceful and attentive, like his mother pouring coffee for her visitors. Despite the fact he knew it was alcohol, Matar couldn't refuse when Gale poured him a glass and raised her own bottle to him. "Welcome, stranger."

He liked how she spoke naturally to him. Without globbing her words as if he were a deaf person. "So where you from? Are you Mexican?"

"Arab."

"Oh, which country?"

"Only. Just. Arabia." He smiled politely, not wanting to become embroiled in geographical explanation. This conversation was turning out to be much more complicated than Matar had anticipated. "English. Me." Here he stabbed his pink waistcoat. "No good."

"Well, that's okay, we don't have to talk." Gale opened

her magazine on the table and the two leaned over together to flip through the saturated color photographs of the Eagle landing on the moon and then leaving orbit again. Matar recognized the awed look on the faces of American kids laid out on living room floors in front of General Electric. He remembered Kuzahmiah's TV and watching the moon landing on the other side of the earth.

By the end of the magazine a wordless familiarity had grown between Gale and Matar. The rolling thunder of bowling-ball-on-pine was too loud to talk over anyway. Eventually, when the rain let up, they stepped out to the wet black curb and a deep orange sunset over the Cascade Mountains. An unlit cigarette hung from her mouth, and her blond hair caught the silvery neon of the sign.

"Hey, how old are you today, anyway?" She spoke thinly through curled lips so as not to drop the cigarette.

"Nineteen," Matar answered.

Gale lit her smoke, hiding her surprise. "Most boys around here only have peach fuzz at nineteen." She flicked her finger along his thick moustache and quickly looked out down Sixth Avenue toward the peak of Mount Rainier. "See that? That's my mountain." She waited for him to respond, but Matar was too absorbed in observing how her light hair ruffled like a static halo around her face. "Do you have mountains like that where you're from in Arabia?"

Matar turned to look at the ice cream colors melting off Rainier's snowcapped peak. Of course there were no mountains like that where he'd come from, but he didn't have the words to explain what there was. It was too much, too big for him, too different from the terrain of his home.

Meanwhile Gale eyed him up and down. His suit was still damp. "We need to find you some better outfits. Where'd you get that nasty suit?" She poked at the horrible spongy polyester just like Matar's mother had.

Matar just shook his head, lightly drunk and unable to explain the morbid backstory. Instead he tugged a little at the strap of her overalls. "What is this?" he asked.

He reminded Gale of a foal nuzzling around for something to eat. "These are overalls."

"All-overs?"

"Overalls. What the farmers wear. You know. No?"

Matar's eyelids were now drooping with exhaustion. Gale guided him back safely to the Ballard Motel, where she showed him how to open the minibar full of snacks. Matar opened and shut the refrigerator door in awe. All this food had been there all along.

"You're a weird one, you know that?" Gale said from the door. "Tell you what, how about I take you to see the mountain tomorrow?" She triangulated a link between the mountain, Matar, and herself to explain before making a driving gesture and pointing back at the fading peak. Of course his answer was yes.

That night, as jet lag kept Matar awake in bed, he remembered the first time he'd heard someone speak English in person. It had been in Kuzahmiah one winter, when a strange truck drove into town. Matar and Mohamed had been sitting in front of their house as a Land Rover pulled up beside the mosque. In it was the first white person Matar had ever seen *not* in black-and-white. He was surprised that he was in fact pink, the same color as the locusts that sometimes blew into their desert from Africa. He loved when they landed in huge swarms, because they were easy to catch, skewer, and roast, and made delicious snacks. The pink man was young and wearing a white *thobe* in the style of city people. He wore a hat to protect his face from the sun and had a leather camera satchel over his shoulder. Matar longed to look inside it. His Saudi guide stepped out of the truck and disappeared into the mosque to ask the imam for directions.

Matar's brother then stood up, long and tall in his charcoal winter *thobe*, and, puffing his chest out, declared, "Watch me speak English." Mohamed strode across the street while Matar watched his brother attempt the dialogue they both knew from the their language-learning book.

Each word was punctuated by a full stop. "Hallo! My. Name. Is. Mohamed!"

Matar watched from a distance as the pink man and Mohamed pantomimed at each other. Mohamed returned with the man in tow and Matar brought out a thermos of tea. The man sat cross-legged on the reed mat, watching as Matar shoveled too much sugar into the already sweetened red tea and stirred nervously.

"Who is your father and your father's father?" he asked Mohamed and Matar in schoolbook Arabic. Mohamed recited their clan's provenance while Matar urged a glass of tea on the man, wishing it were already cold since he knew that's how the cowboys drank it.

The man took notes, excitedly writing the names down in a little notebook. Then he looked around in his bag for something to give the boys and produced a can of Pepsi, a blue pencil, and a blank notebook full of graph paper. He

THE GIRL WHO FELL TO EARTH

gave the notebook to Matar and the can of Pepsi to Mohamed. By now the man's Saudi guide was back in the truck
and honked the horn, calling, "Mister Stark! *Yalla!* I'll take
you to the Bedouin camp now."

The pink man rose and said *"Ma'a salama"* to both boys,
and just like that, the young anthropologist was gone. Matar
sparked with a desperate wish to stop the Land Rover as it
drove off. Later he would recognize the feeling as one that
plagued everyone in the tribe. It was the urge to move on.
Now as he lay in his dank motel room, tangled in super-
fluous sheets and an uncomfortably soft mattress, all Matar
wanted to do was go back. The *khayal* from his boyhood
returned, a ghostly smudge with its reflective face, standing
guard in his periphery, holding a vigil until Matar slept and
dreamed of his impossibly distant home.

Gale returned early the next morning to Matar's hotel room.
He opened the door in his *sirwal*, wearing the thermal blanket as a cape and still looking like a very lost little boy. "I
brought you these." Gale invited herself in and heaved a pile
of clothes onto the bed: Wranglers and Levi's and button-up
cotton madras with pearly buttons. "You can get rid of that
salmon disco ensemble." She made a beeline for the refrigerator, picked out a can of Rainier, stuck her thumb in to
crack the push-button top of the can, and sucked the froth
off her thumb. Matar stood stunned in the threshold of his
hotel room, half in and half out of more secondhand duds.

"So? You ready for your birthday present? Come on, let's
go," she said, pounding down the rest of her can and charg-
ing out to her gold Volkswagen Scirocco.

He wavered a few seconds before letting go of the horrible empty feeling that came when she left, and followed her out to her car. First she drove him down to the waterfront naval yards where cargo and battleships towered as high as the adjacent hills. Matar began to get panicky as she drove up close to the piers.

"What's the matter?" she asked.

"No. Water," he tried to explain. She stepped out and walked down the pier, gazing out across the bay; it was clear and calm and the brimstone stench from the paper mill was mild that day. "Just have a look at it, will you?" she called to Matar. But he refused to look or even get out of the car. "All right, then, we'll head straight for the hills."

They drove away from the shore, Matar calming down the farther they drove, eased by the peace of movement. She took the scenic route to the mountain. Windows rolled down, hair in the wind, a pair of leather driving gloves, and an 8-track of *Waylon and Willie* all the way. Gale stopped at the Indian reservation for more smokes, and Matar perused the cartoon-colored fireworks. She drove up and up into the hills, driving always toward the peak that never seemed to move from their view. The mountain was like Samira's TV eyes; no matter where he went, there it was, looming down at him.

"You. Drive. Good." Matar gave Gale an approving thumbs-up.

"You are a good driver," she corrected him and he repeated. "Why, thank you, sir. I am flattered," Gale replied to his grammatically correct compliment.

The old cowboys' haggard voices sang in tandem again,

"If you don't understand him, an' he don't die young / He'll prob'ly just ride away."

After a while Matar gathered up a thought worth trying to explain. "Inside the airplane. I thought the sun, he was run away from me." Matar illustrated his panicked in-flight anxiety with hand gestures for "airplane" and "sun" and "run away."

"You were coming west. You were flying with the night." Gale fisted one gloved hand and demonstrated with the other how the plane moved around it. Matar lurched to grab the wheel as they started to career. She tried to pull the gloves off with her teeth to explain better and fanned her fingers out over Matar's lap. "Help me out here, will ya?" she insisted, using her other hand to steer. He obeyed, tugging at each finger of the glove gently and removing it. The elastic seams had left pink trails on her skin, crisscrossing blue veins, like a map.

That night, high up in the mountains, they lay back on the hood of Gale's gold Scirocco. A full moon was rising over the zigzag outline of pine forest that stacked the foothills. There was no light pollution up here and the stars came out, though not as brightly as they did in the desert. Matar pointed out the names of stars in Arabic to Gale, and this time she repeated after him.

"Al-Dheeb."

"The Wolf."

"*Gumar.*"

"Moon," Gale returned. "Can you see the man's face in the *gumar*?"

"No. He is the rabbit," Matar disagreed matter-of-factly.

"Honey. I hate to break it to you, but that is a man," retorted Gale, angling her elbow up on the windshield and turning to look at him.

"It is the rabbit," he insisted, and the gold hood of the Scirocco dented under his weight. Many things were new and confusing to Matar, but of the big bunny in the moon he was sure.

"What if it could be both?"

Matar remained sitting upright, wound up at this contradiction to everything he knew to be true. Gale lay back, tickled by how upset he'd gotten, and winked to calm him down.

Matar's gut jumped and he fought the urge to look behind him to make sure she was winking at him and not his brother. "Yes. It can," he decided. "You see that star?" he asked, and pointed out the steady prick of light, westernmost in the First Leap. "This star, she is belong to me."

Gale slid closer to him on the hood of the car and leaned in close. "I've got a mountain and you've got a star. Now all we need is a rocket ship and we're good to go!"

4

ETA ERIDANI •
THE HATCHING PLACE • اشيانة

Gale had grown up on a farm in the Puyallup Valley. Her
mother, Sophia Valo, still lived on the farm, cradled between
two hills rowed with thick stands of black-green Douglas
fir. They were flanked on all sides by a ripple of kept raspberry tines and wild blackberry brambles; the thorny lattice
of roots and briars were all that held the dirt from washing away in the drench of Northwest rain. After a several-
month-long road trip together, Gale finally invited Matar to
visit the farm she had grown up on. Playing pool in roadside
taverns and learning how to navigate the big freeways of the
Northwest turned out to be far more educational than any
language class could have been for Matar.

The fact that Gale's mother and his own mother, Safya,
had such similar names was an odd bit of serendipity, and
because of it he wanted to pay Sophia appropriate tribute.
He decided a lamb would be most appropriate for the occasion, and bought one from a farmer in the nearby hills.
Strapped into the passenger side of the Scirocco, the lamb
blinked and sniffed around the leather seat. Matar patted her
head while she strained against the safety belt and bopped

her muzzle on the glass landscape whizzing by. He was looking forward to eating *kepsa* as much as he was to impressing Gale and Sophia with his mother's recipe. Before presenting the lamb to Sophia, Gale tied a shiny yellow ribbon around her neck. He thought it was strange, but he'd seen dogs with sweaters and cats with jewelry since coming to America, so he accepted that a lamb with a ribbon must be some bizarre local custom.

"What a sweetheart," Sophia exclaimed, lifting the sniffly little thing up into her arms. "You did good," Gale whispered to Matar while Sophia rocked the little lamb in her arms and took Matar on a tour of the house. She showed him the toolshed full of bow saws and sickles, the cellar full of raspberry preserves and pickles, and the out-of-tune pump organ she had saved from the neighbor's chicken coop.

For Matar, Sophia and Gale's home was a cave of wonders. It was full of interesting things to look at, and even though it was spare by American standards, Matar was overwhelmed with the amount of *stuff* Gale had grown up surrounded by. There were shelves full of books, and a clock in every room. There were *two* freezers: one for preserving excess berries and one for normal use. The hearth over the fireplace was covered with Space Needle souvenirs, a fully rigged ship in a bottle, and a pretty stone globe marked 1915 at its base. Among all these mementos, pride of place was given to a portrait of Gale's father and Sophia's husband, Charles, or Kaarle, as he was known when he arrived in America. At fourteen he'd left Finland as a cabin boy. Four years later, after four trips across the equator, Kaarle went ashore at San Francisco to attend the World's

Fair and never went back to sea again. In the photo over the hearth he was eighteen years old and about eighteen years late to the gold rush, posing with pan and shovel before a sign bearing the tourism slogan "Klondike or Bust!" Sophia didn't put the lamb down until she went to bed, when she reluctantly tied her to the porch rail.

The next morning Matar woke early to prepare his gift. He unknotted the rope from the cast-iron railing where Sophia had tethered the lamb. Her knobby knees wobbled in the mud as he strode easily across the tractor ruts of the field in the direction of the river. Sophia was boiling a pot of coffee at the kitchen window when she caught sight of a streak of yellow disappearing at the border of the field. She went to wake Gale, worried someone was stealing her lamb. When he reached the sandbank, Matar removed the ribbon from around her curly neck, closed his eyes, and, pointing his thumb, guessed at a line to Mecca. Then, in a few expert swoops, he laid the lamb down on her left side, hand over her eyes, knees holding down her legs. He held the back of her neck in a strong grip for a few moments, then said, *"BismAllah. AllahhuAkbar,"* and slit the lamb's throat along the bottom of her skull. He waited a minute or two, letting the blood pool in the sand and dribble down into a sinkhole by the river. When the blood slowed down, he hacked the rest of the way through the muscle and spine at the neck and the little body went into convulsions, nerves ending across the body.

When he came back up the hill and across the field, Gale and Sophia were both standing on the porch. They reminded him of his mother perched on a desert cliff waiting for him to return with the goats. She'd always seemed to him like a great black bird when she kept this vigil, watching the horizon for her herd to appear. As he approached, Matar saw the horror on their faces. Sophia took one look at the limp lamb over his shoulder and went inside, slamming the porch door behind her.

"I know you meant well," Gale said as Matar wiped his bloodied hands in the grass. "Heck, Mom used to break chicken's necks by swinging them over her head. Who knew she had such a soft spot for lambs?" An exclamation of blood squirted out of the lamb's open neck as if to punctuate her sentence.

Gale disappeared into the house to comfort her mother. Matar set about the skinning; he wasn't going to leave the job half done. He tied the body upside down by one leg from the porch rail and lifted the membrane to make small, loosening cuts. The skin came away from the muscle easily and he wound the hanging piece of skin and wool around his hand as he pulled it away. For the first time since meeting Gale, he felt lost.

After starting out on the wrong foot with Sophia, Matar was determined to make it up. When he proved incapable of certain gardening tasks—how did she expect someone from the desert to know the difference between weeds and vegetables?—he started driving her around town on errands. He and Sophia made an odd pairing as they appeared together around Puyallup in Sophia's Ford Galaxie. The car hadn't been taken out in almost a decade, and in recent years Sophia had become increasingly reclusive, so her sudden arrival with a foreigner piqued the interest of people in town.

Sophia was prim, hair teased up in a soft white permanent, and Matar was young, dark, and floppy-haired. At the store Matar took the stern of the metal basket while Sophia led him around the wide aisles by its prow. Purse over arm and scribbled list in hand, she navigated the supermarket efficiently, handing cans and jars back to Matar so he could practice reading. After his Tide mistake, he was very keen to learn to identify food by its packaging. Since he'd grown up foraging for breakfast, the cereal section gave Matar vertigo. Strolling through Piggly Wiggly was the starkest reminder of how far he was from home; the bounty of the supermarket overwhelmed Matar.

As they pushed past the meat refrigerator, yellow light on bloody Styrofoam, Sophia prodded at him with a hint of vindictiveness, "So. What do they have for dinner where you're from? Besides *innocent* baby lambs, that is."

He thought better of telling her about camel, lizard, or locust. "Rice."

Sophia poked at a ham through its plastic and chucked it into the cart. "So, no pig, then?"

"No," Matar confirmed, eyeing the meat in the basket. "The pig, he is not clean."

They passed an open door where a butcher was carving up and weighing pieces of a hog. The countertop was thatched with cleaver marks and gritty with gristle and guts. Sophia had walked by this scene thousands of times, but she could see Matar was disturbed at both the meat and the method. She placed the honey ham she'd selected back into the open fridge. "I have a hankering for some fried rice tonight," she declared.

Matar and Sophia continued to forge a bond over the following months. Twice a week he visited Sophia, and they watched *Mork and Mindy* together. The running joke between them was that if he could comprehend Robin Williams's fast talk he could understand anyone in English. Most of the jokes went over his head, but he learned the rhythm of the humor and how to laugh on cue.

One afternoon Matar noticed that Gale's car was gone from the carport, nothing but an oil spot marking the place it should have been.

"Where is Gale?" he asked just as Mork put in a call to Orson for his weekly report. Sophia turned the TV down.

"She's gone for a checkup at the doctor. She'll be back soon." She patted her fluffy hair, which reminded him of unspun wool, and sighed loudly. "You got brothers and sisters, Matar?" she asked. This was the first time she had asked him directly about his family.

"Yes. Eleven."

"Well, I'll be." Sophia slumped back in her chair, amazed. "Your poor mother!"

Matar caught a piece of drift from his memory. It must have been before his family had stopped moving, before they lost their way and stopped being nomads. He was small, three or four years old, and he could not sleep for his mother's screaming. She heaved down over the great lump of her pregnancy, and all that separated her from her frightened children was a thin flap of tent wool. Matar's father, Jabir, came in and out of the tent with clean sand gathered in the skirt of his *thobe* and dumped it between his wife's legs. Blankets and fabric were hard to come by, so sand was

the most practical way for him to sop up the blood. Jabir
mounded it into a sort of sand-cradle for the baby to fall
into. A rope swung from the tent pole, and Matar saw her
crane up, wrists wrapped to whiteness in the coils as the
new baby passed downwards, head crowning in the sky over
the miniature dunes heaped between Safya's thighs. Though
this early memory was vivid and clear, Matar had no words
to speak of it . . . in any language.

"You all right there, Matar?" Sophia put her hand on his
shoulder.

The conversation was now trumping the alien in rainbow suspenders. Mindy sent Mearth, their half-human,
half-extra-terrestrial offspring, upstairs to bed and Sophia
switched the TV to PBS, where Carl Sagan was handing
photographs from the *Voyager 1* spacecraft out to a classroom of kids.

"Do you ever think about having children yourself?"

Matar sensed a certain seriousness in her question, but
the answer was simple. "Of course," he said. Having children
was an obvious inevitability to him, as was marriage, Hajj,
death, and resurrection on *Yawm Al-Qiyamah*.

Sophia seemed pleased with this affirmative answer and
reached out to pat his hand. "You and Gale come from different worlds, but just so you know, you're okay with me."

Matar wasn't sure what these sudden proclamations of
fondness were about, but he was on the cusp of guessing.
Even though this was small talk on a night just like their
other evenings spent watching the spaceman who hatched
from an egg, there was something in the weight of Sophia's
hand that was giving him a very clear hint. But before Matar

could piece it all together, they heard the Scirocco lurch into the carport, alerting them in unison like a nervous pair of prairie dogs. Gale burst in the back door and put her hands on her hips.

"Well, guess what?" It was a rhetorical question. Matar and Sophia both knew what she was going to say before she said it. "I'm pregnant."

BETA PERSEI • THE GHOUL • الغول

The fact that I am a bastard child was kept from me and probably would have remained a secret if I hadn't found photographic proof. The incriminating picture was taken on my parents' wedding day. We are clustered together on top of the Space Needle. Gale, my mother, wears her silver silk wedding dress with a baby's-breath wreath; Matar, my father, wears a blue suit and has a beard. My newlywed parents cradle me between them as if I were a chubby flightless bird, diapered and plumed with an impressive display of lace. My tiny brown face is frozen in an ugly twist of discomfort that probably had as much to do with trapped wind as it did with the cold gusts on the observation deck. Matar's and Gale's eyebrows are raised in wild grins. This desperate amazement makes them look like they just won me in a game show. In the bottom right corner is an orange date stamp; it took me a minute to notice it was a year later than I'd been led to believe. This evidence of my illegitimacy was shuffled into the bottom of an unmarked box with old passport photos, landscape doubles, water-damaged paperbacks, and old movie ticket stubs. Someone had obviously tried to make it disappear.

Apparently I was a fussy baby, and around the time of their marriage, my parents discovered that the enveloping darkness of the movie theater was a very effective way of putting me to sleep. How they managed to figure out the soporific effects of surround-sound Vangelis is a mystery. Whatever the story, we attended many of the hits of the day as a family, including *Tron*, *Blade Runner*, and *E.T.*, as well as reruns like *Jaws*, *Westworld*, and *Close Encounters of the Third Kind* that played for half-price on Monday nights, according to the stubs in the box I found. Ma had seen *Close Encounters* when it first came out in 1977 and had loved it. But having a child in her arms the second time around heightened the abduction scene for her.

"This is spookier than I remember it," she said, shifting uneasily in her seat at the movie theater. "Can we go?" But Matar wasn't listening, and just patted her hand. "I left with you when you wanted to leave *Jaws*," she hissed at him vindictively. Someone in the darkness shushed her. "I'll be in the car." She picked me up and followed the pinprick lights up the aisle and back out into the daylight, leaving Matar, his mouth hanging open as Melinda Dillon went screaming into a field, colored lights disappearing into the rolling sky.

The second daylight hit my face I woke up and started to bawl. The only other way to get me to sleep was to strap me into my car seat, put a hat on me, and drive. Whenever Ma pressed the brake I'd start up the wailing again, so she kept the Scirocco in motion, circling the crowded parking lot and waiting for the movie to be over. She turned on the radio to distract herself. A talk show came on the air about the subject of kidnapping. One of the guests was a woman from

Texas who was invited to tell the frightening account of her son's brutal kidnapping by his father.

A drawling voice on the radio said, "Well, me and Ali were running together a few months and then one day, outta nowhere, he just disappeared until a few years later, when I ran into him with some of his old friends. By then my little boy Frankie had black hair and looked just like his daddy. It was obvious."

The woman started to sob, and Gale rolled down the window for a cigarette.

"He says he's here to take my little Frank to his *real* family. That he's going to be a prince over in Arabia somewhere." Ma's cigarette burned down to the stub and blew off without her noticing. "They said that because I wasn't married to Frankie's daddy I had no right over his custody. I dunno, maybe if I'd married him I'd be a queen somewh—"

Gale killed the radio. In a few years, Betty Mahmoudy's *Not Without My Daughter* would cause a buzz and the "Invasion of the Muslim Baby Snatchers" would climax briefly as a hot topic on daytime talk shows. Gale's instinct had never been to marry Matar. Until this story, she had assumed her hand was the upper one in the relationship. She had wanted children. That was all. Only now did she reflect on how little she knew about Matar's family, or how little he'd been able to articulate in English about the world he came from. And that had been just fine—until now. Perhaps things would be more complicated than she'd planned for us.

For all she knew, Matar could be part of some larger genetic conspiracy to spawn with blond American women and then rob them of their offspring. Thoughts like this began circling Gale's mind like paranoid vultures. She drove in a circuit outside the cinema, waiting for the aliens and the Americans to have their cosmic jam session. She had smoked a whole pack of Marlboros by the time Matar emerged from the theater, squinting. White American families poured out around him, talking animatedly in a shared language about the possibility of making contact with the other worlds. To Gale, Matar couldn't have been stranger.

"Doo. Doo. Doo. Dee. Doo." Matar whistled the inter-planetary jingle as he slid into the passenger seat. He leaned over, smiling, to kiss Gale.

"Don't do that!" she snapped. "Have you told your family about us?"

This question blindsided Matar. "Why you make problems? They don't know where I am, even."

"Good," she said and began to drive through the herd of townsfolk exiting the theater.

Matar quietly buckled his seat belt and checked that I was strapped in as the car lurched and braked with Ma's agitation. "Why you are asking these question?"

She gassed it around the back of the cinema along the river. "What would your family say if they knew about us?"

"They would want to see our daughter."

"Would they want to see *me*?"

Matar paused, measuring how to say the wise thing. "Yes, if you became a Muslim and we got married. Why not?"

"And if I was not a Muslim?"

"Why you are thinking like this way?" She parked the car again, having just driven a large circle around the cinema and come back to where she had started.

Then, like gentling an upset animal, Matar leaned across and held the back of her neck like he did when calming a lamb. "Will you marry me?"

Matar had wanted an Islamic wedding presided over by an imam, but that was a tall order in Puyallup. When there was no one to marry a Bedouin couple in the desert, they just circled a tree, commanding it three times with the words, "You! Tree! Marry us!" and then got down to business. So Matar agreed to a trade-off with Gale: in exchange for a simple nondenominational ceremony, Gale would quietly convert to Islam and raise their children as Muslims. In the end, the marriage consisted of a civil ceremony performed by a notary public in the kitchen of the farmhouse, and, later that evening when the newlyweds were alone, a private circumnavigation of a lilac bush in the backyard.

Having a child out of wedlock or even marrying outside the tribe might easily be forgiven, but marrying outside the religion was bound to pose an issue for Matar. If he got Gale to say the *shahada*, just two little statements, it would change everything. The only problem was that, like the kiss of true love breaking the spell on a sleeping beauty, if Gale was going to say "*La ilaha ilAllah wa Mohamed al Rasul Allah*," she was going to have to not only understand but also *mean* the words "There is no God but God and Mohamed is his prophet."

He set about composing instruction cards with the different *rakat* for Gale to perform during the five prayer times and recorded himself reading Quran on cassette tapes. Now their roles were reversed. Gale had been Matar's guide to

America; Matar was now stepping in to guide her toward Islam. Eventually, Gale grudgingly agreed to try to pray if Matar agreed to learn to swim. To Gale, being able to float was a survival skill necessary for fatherhood, just as being Muslim was an essential part of motherhood to Matar. It seemed like a fair and equal trade to both parties.

It was around this time that Gale found she was pregnant again. This pregnancy came with two recurrent ordeals. The first was a tormenting anxiety dream about alien abduction in the wake of watching *Close Encounters*; the second was a craving for pickled pigs' feet, which Matar found repulsive. She would sit upright in the night, eyes jabbing the back of her lids, thrashing in the sheets, and grab for me to make sure I was still there. Then she'd shuffle to the kitchen, root through the refrigerator, and fish a hoof out of a jar of brine with her fingers. Matar would catch her there in the cold light, confiscate the jar, and lead her back to bed.

"When you are afraid, recite the Verse of the Throne and you will feel brave," he said.

Gale rebuffed him and shoved a breast into my face for my morning feed. "It's simple, darling—when you learn how to swim, I'll learn how to pray."

The Puyallup pool belonged to the valley's high school and was relatively empty on Sundays. "Where is the lifeman?" Matar asked nervously as they padded barefoot across the damp tiles.

"Lifeguards are off Sunday. We have it to ourselves!" Gale sat on the edge of the pool, baby bump protruding far over her thighs as she dipped me in and out of the tepid water like a biscuit. "Come on, sit down here next to me," she coaxed

Matar. He just flicked at the water with his big toe. "Don't be stupid. Get in!" She tried wrestling his leg with her free arm until he climbed timidly down the ladder and slipped hip-deep into the pool.

Walking Matar through all the basic lessons—how to breathe out under water, how to float, how to tread water, and how to kick—Gale coaxed him to the deep end.

"Okay, now swim back. No wall!"

But Matar refused to leave the wall of the pool, bobbing along the length of the twenty-five-meter lane with his hands on the ledge. "*Khalas!* I am finish!" Matar called back.

Fed up, Gale stood and hoisted me onto her hip over where Matar was clinging to a railing, trying to catch his breath.

"Do you know how my father taught me to swim?" she asked. Matar shook his head and blew his nose. "Like this!" My mother tossed me into the deep end of the pool, a little over a meter from where Matar was hanging on for dear life. I bobbed easily to the surface, and by the time my father had reached me I was floating comfortably on my back.

He barely made it back to the side of the pool and handed me up to my mother. "You crazy?" he sputtered, and it echoed off the bleachers.

Ma ignored his sputters and toweled me off.

"You wants your daughter she drown?" Matar was losing his proper English skills in his fury.

"It's fine, darling. She knows how to swim. Babies are born with it."

Matar refused to believe Gale and would not be pacified even when she showed him my infant back-float skills in a full bathtub. Even today when the story of Ma letting me drop into the pool comes up, my father gets angry.

That night he kept his back to her in bed.

"You still want to teach me how to pray?" she asked in an attempt at making up.

His stony shadow softened, and he turned over to spoon her. "You frighten me today."

"But you faced your fear. That was the right thing."

Matar leaned in to whisper into her ear, in Arabic, "I seek refuge in Allah from the outcast Satan."

Gale repeated after him, *"Authu Bi Allah min al Shaytan al rajim,"* stumbling on the hard consonants and mispronouncing words, but Matar didn't correct her or explain to her what she was saying. Instead he gently continued this way until the verse was completed.

"Do you feel more safe now?" he asked her, noticing that the rise and fall of her breathing had slowed. She said yes with a sleepy silence and guided his hand to a spot on her abdomen where a little foot was straining against the skin.

They lay together like this for a long time until Matar felt the time was right. "There is no God but God and Mohamed is his prophet," he said softly into her ear.

"La ilaha ilAllah wa Mohamed al Rasul Allah," Gale repeated. Matar basked in his triumph and went to kiss his newly Muslim wife, but was instead he was greeted by a soft snore as she drew her next breath.

6

BETA CEPHEI • THE FLOCK • الفرق

Before my sister Dima was born, our father Matar had made numerous forays into the profession of long-haul trucking. He liked the big rigs. Even though they were cab-over-engine Macks, not Mercedes, they still reminded him of home. He added flourishes to his English by listening to the crass lilt of CB lingo and UFO conspiracy-theory sermons. He managed to get freelance work from a few contacts he'd made at the Port of Tacoma. Without his own cab it was hard to get jobs. Still, no one could deny that if they needed a long, straight trek at a steady pace, the *Ayrab* could do it.

For Matar it was also an excuse to see more of America, to drive far from all the cities, where he could see the starlight. It was also the only way to quell that old urge to keep moving.

While Matar was tearing up and down the I-5, Gale had worked straight through both pregnancies as a meter reader in Tacoma. But when she took up wearing *hijab*, her employers at the city found that the sight of her in a veil poking around electrical meters in people's backyards was giving customers the creeps. They gave her the choice to remove it or lose the job.

It was then that Baba decided it was time for him to return to the Gulf. With Abu Dhabi, Doha, and the entire region transforming rapidly in the sway of a great black gold rush, he decided to light out for his old territories. He figured he'd have a pretty good shot at a well-paying job, especially now that he could speak English with the big men in charge of the oil companies. He promised he'd send for us once everything was settled, but there was no way of knowing when that might be.

It had been three years since Matar had come to America. He'd explored the country, married a native, and fathered two kids, and yet somehow he managed to leave with no baggage. We dropped him off at the airport with the same nearly empty leather briefcase he'd arrived with. Nothing inside it but his *sirwal* and a *thobe* to change into when he landed. Ma tucked a photo into his wallet of the four of us at the Space Needle in Seattle, Ma and Baba bowed together over Dima and me. Our father left almost everything he'd accumulated over the years behind with us. Our closet remained packed with his shirts and the Quran tapes he'd recorded for us. Too young to really remember him, we knew his smell without knowing who it belonged to, and knew his voice before we'd ever spoken to him.

I must have been nearly five years old when we finally received word from our father. He sent us a package that included a videotape, a studio portrait of himself, and some corporate gift pens. "That's your babi." Ma introduced us and let Dima smudge the framed photo with her fingers. Of course it wasn't a proper studio portrait; it had been taken for work. Or so it would seem, judging by the Japanese company logo and the photo of a flaming offshore rig erupting over his left shoulder. He sat stiffly, as if he'd been holding the pose for a long time. It reminded me of the photo on the mantel of our Grandfather Kaarle standing with a "Klondike or Bust!" banner as his backdrop.

A letter was taped to the back of the photo frame.

Dear my dotters,
This fideo from your Baba in dawha.
Your family they wants see you.
You have 11 auntie and uncles in dawha and your
Gramma and Grampa they are in Saudia
Also you have too many cousins.
We wait you and miss you too much.
Next year come. And if you can like it stay.
My wife,
I miss you and America also. Donot forgit your prey.
Promis. I love you honne. Baba Matar

Next we settled down to watch Baba's tape. Ma pulled Dima up onto her lap, and I sat too close to the TV, squinting through my plastic-frame glasses. When the static drew back on the screen, we heard men speaking in Baba's language. The view was of the color beige, a speeding shot from a car in the desert.

Ma recognized one of the voices as Matar. "There's your baba's voice. I'll bet he's forgotten all of his English."

The microphone crackled from the wind as the camera spun around to face our father.

"Welcome my girls!" he said.

Ma put her hand over her mouth to hide her smile.

"This is our country road. You can see your new home. Lots to see!" He turned the camera around to capture the car's approach to the Doha Sheraton, an iconic structure jutting from an outcrop at the edge of the city. "This is new. When I met you, Gale, it was not here," Baba shouted into the wind. They pulled up slowly alongside a line of Ferraris and other fancy cars parked in front of the lobby. "This is my new car," he said, pointing the camera at a gleaming DeLorean parked under a palm tree. Ma laughed. My eyes widened. "Sorry. Joking. Your Baba's not rich . . . *yet.*"

He took us inside. The lobby was a seductive Islamic fantasy-future of hexagonal mirrors and disco-lit elevators. My eyes widened. It was beautiful. At the center of the lobby was the largest standing chandelier in the world: a crystal palm tree. We exited to the garden, where the camera panned briefly over Indian men gardening on a path beside a giant chessboard. He pointed the camera out to the water. "You cannot believe it, Gale. Now I am working on a rig, way far out there in the sea. I'm not afraid anymore of the water." He demonstrated by patting his bare foot in the seawater for Ma's benefit, and she responded by hugging Dima. Back in the car he pointed the camera at himself again. "Everything is changing here now, Gale."

The video carried on for a few minutes out the window of the old car—which drove at warp speed past lonely vistas of desert—as though he'd forgotten to turn it off. Then suddenly he said, "Tell the girls I love them very much."

"They know," Ma replied to the TV, a choke in her throat as the black slug at the end of the tape doused the image.

That videotape was a revelation to me, and as the white noise resumed I saw it as a portal into another dimension—one I felt immediate ownership over, if only because I had been told it was mine. Having a second world to belong to immediately made me cast doubt on my place in the first. It seemed like such a very different world from the rivers and the raspberry farm. I can't say it was exotic, or mysterious, or any of the other alluring adjectives associated with the Gulf. But seeing the video permanently cracked the world into two halves for me. I watched and re-watched the tape so many times the belt wore out. It made me feel funny, a new yearning, like my mind was salivating for something new. I wanted to go there as soon as I could. Maybe it was as simple as missing my father; either way, Ma was forced by the video to acknowledge that we would never be fully hers. Eventually her daughters would have to learn to live in both worlds.

A few evenings later, while Dima and I were parked in front of *Cosmos* watching the man in the red turtleneck and camel jacket explain tesseracts, Ma called us to the telephone. "Girls! Come talk to your baba!" She sat in the kitchen in jeans and one of his old shirts. She had her *hijab* down on her shoulders, and her wrists were tangled up from nervously twisting the phone cord. Ma scooped Dima up to her lap, where she held the phone to my little sister's ear. "Say *salam alaikum, Baba*." Dima's fat cheek pillowed against the receiver. She breathed heavily into the phone but didn't say anything. I clawed my way up onto Ma's lap, wedging myself into range for my turn. *"Asalam alaikum?"* I showed off, holding the receiver to my face.

"Safya! Will you like to come and live with your baba?"

"Can we fly there?"

"Yes."

"In a airplane?"

"Yes."

"Do we have to go through outer space to get there?"

Ma cuffed me. "Don't be silly. This is a long-distance phone call."

"No, but you do fly over the North Pole," he answered.

"Go help your Gramma in the garden," Ma scolded.

I ran out to tell Gramma, who was hosing down the rhododendrons in her muumuu and boots. "We're going to see Babi in Doha!" I yelled across the yard at her.

"You kids might as well be flying to the moon for all I know," she grumbled, and kinked the hose off.

We set out for Qatar a month later. The problematic nature of our situation in the Gulf was not made clear to Ma until the London-to-Dhahran leg of our trip, where she made easy transit-friends with Aramco oil wives in the smoking section at the rear of the plane. Ma stuck out among all the white linen, tan faces, and bleach-blond hair, her *hijab* and morning-glory dress making her look severe and unfriendly to the other American ladies. "I guess you don't drink anymore then, huh?" one asked, directing a dismissive gesture at the *hijab* on Ma's head. Ma took it in stride and shared her pack of Marlboros around. The most boisterous among them was a woman named Mary Lou. She was from Kansas, and one thing was certain—she didn't want to go back to Saudi, because "there really *is* no place like home."

It was on that flight that Ma learned being an expat American woman and being married to an Arab meant that although she and these women came from the same backgrounds, they were bound into two very different worlds. The gap between Ma and Mary Lou could not have been wider. Ma was the wife of a Bedouin man, the kind Mary Lou's husband thought of as a coolie. Mary Lou was wife to the kind of man who had the power to drill any of Al-Dafira's land and yet thought twice about hiring Bedouin. Mary Lou explained all of this and more to Ma while drinking her gin and tonics somewhere over Jordan.

"I tell ya, Gale, it's a different *planet* over there. You don't know what you're getting yourself into." Before Ma could get a word in edgewise, Mary Lou grabbed her by the knee and leaned forward in a conspiratorial (drunk) whisper: "My husband works with a guy who makes his wives sleep three to a bed!"

"I don't think you're in any position to judge," Ma said, hoping it would be the last word. Mary Lou raised a penciled eyebrow. "Don't kid yourself, sweetie." And swilling the ice in her cup, she knocked it all back. "They're all the same. *Ayrabs.*"

Ma watched Mary Lou stagger back to her seat. A steward came over and crouched down to speak with Ma. "I just want you to know, we see this all the time on this flight," he assured her. "I hope she didn't offend you. They usually have to get drunk to go willingly."

When the plane stopped in Dhahran, an officer came aboard to check the passports of everyone going to Doha. He looked through Ma's passport, bored, and then opened mine and Dima's. He did a double take at the last name Al-Dafira before calling for another officer to come and gawk at the white woman with the Bedouin children. The plane filled up around us with Indian men transiting through Doha to Mumbai or Kerala.

It was the middle of the night by the time we landed on the tarmac in Doha. Ma stood out like an alien at the top of the steps. Two men stood at the foot of the stairs, long hair protruding from under their checkered *gutras*. There was something familiar about their manner. "They were like your father," she'd tell me years later when I asked about our first passage to the Gulf. "I don't know how, but they let me know." One of them gently relieved Ma of Dima while the other took me by the hand, leaving Ma to carry her bag. For a moment she panicked; these were strangers. But as if he had read her thoughts, the man holding my hand traded me for her bag.

They whisked us through a special line at passport control, and on the other side Baba stood at the baggage carousel. The two men each kissed him on the nose (a practice Ma complained about as being "kind of fruity"), and we waited our turn in the pecking order of "hello." Baba knelt down to kiss Dima and me, and then rose to tell Ma hello, but she intercepted him with a long, bold kiss, shocking the few stragglers in the terminal. Baba tried to hide his grin as he reprimanded Ma for the benefit of his cousins and led us out to his car, which was not, to my dismay, the DeLorean. It took a long time to get from the airport to our new home. Dima and I watched from the backseat as we passed through the pockmarked moonscape of construction pits and cranes that was our new home.

"Close your eyes!" Baba flung the door open on Apartment 1303. We closed our eyes in the hallway and waited for him to give us the cue. "Come here. No, here. Okay. Open!" We stood in a wide marble hallway with five closed doors.

"Which one is ours?" Ma asked, scanning the doorframes for numbers.

"Ha!" Baba was pleased with her country-mouse mistake. He opened each of the heavy doors and proclaimed, "All of them!" The rooms were dark and empty, and cold air gusted out of them like a chill wafting up from some subterranean river.

"Do all the A/Cs have to be on at once?" Ma stomped into the darkness and turned off the rumbling air conditioner. Her astonishment at the size of the flat turned to suspicion as she saw that the room was lined with floor-to-ceiling mirrors. "Matar. How can we afford this? You could fit *two* families in here."

It was not the reaction he'd been hoping for. "Bah. Don't worry. I have it all under control."

But Ma knew by his sheepish lack of eye contact that he most definitely did not. The cavernous rooms and creepy stillness of un-lived-in living spaces dampened the thrill of being with our father. Ma investigated further, flicking the lights on and off in each room as if to check if something might be lurking. We went into the living room, which was dominated by a huge pane of glass framing a view of the water. Light from the construction cranes dimly frosted the room. Ma and Baba stood together in silhouette beside a large telescope. Ma bent to have a look at where it pointed: a rig out at sea. She lifted me up to see the red flame glimmering in the scope. It was shockingly detailed, the ripples on the water, the jutting trunk of the rig, and the flame itself. It was like looking closely at a perfectly rendered miniature.

"That's where Baba works," she said to me.

"I go back tomorrow morning," Baba announced.

"But it's Saturday!"

"Yes, the weekend is Thursday and Friday."

Exhausted from the journey, she didn't have it in her to mask disappointment.

"Don't worry. Your new family will be here to visit in a few days."

Ma slumped into a chair. "We came an awful long way for you to leave us again."

Baba changed the subject. "I have one more surprise for you!" He coaxed Ma out of her chair and took us back to the elevator, which took us to a mezzanine floor. "This had better be good if you're going to strand us," Ma said, following behind us as we came out to an open rooftop lined with plastic sun chairs.

"Pool!" I yelped, and ran for the kidney-shaped hole in the middle of the seventh-story patio.

"For swimming lessons," he said, and Ma softened a little as he hugged her to him.

We spent the following week settling in. Ma locked the extra rooms. The longer they remained locked, the more dread gathered around them. They were like the forbidden attic of some neo-Gothic romance set in the Gulf, neglected ghosts lurking in the brightly lit wings of our glass castle.

She filled the shelves with the books she had brought for us, including the Laura Ingalls Wilder books and a mini-library of abridged, illustrated English classics: *Treasure Island*, *The Swiss Family Robinson*, and *The Jungle Book* among them. On the top shelf she kept a medical dictionary full of explicit photos of rashes and parasites, alongside which she kept her copy of Frank Herbert's *Dune* for her own amusement. We spent a lot of time at the pool in the early mornings, where Dima bobbed in water wings and Ma instructed me on how to dive with as little splash as possible into the pool.

"Tuck your head in!" she'd call from her umbrella, where she watched me show off my headstands and push Dima around the little blue hole with her water wings and inner tube.

At night Ma swiveled the telescope on its tripod and squinted out at the horizon. She reminded me of a queen from one of our illustrated classics, trapped in a turret, surveying her new realm. We took turns looking out at the little candle on the sea. The water of the Gulf was often still, like silver jelly. The only spots of ripple were where three-meter concrete jacks were being dumped into the shallows to build new islands shaped like pearls and palm trees. Beyond the gravel barges, past the rot-bottomed dhows and the nets that kept hammerheads away from the beach, was the unfocused quiver of flame where our father worked. But that little flame in the night was tantalizingly close after we'd traveled so far.

Baba's schedule was such that he would get one week onshore for every three weeks offshore. We would spend those three weeks in a strange limbo watching Grendizer, the translated Japanese space robot, on television and going for walks on the corniche, a waterside promenade studded with fountains and star-shaped gazebos. Efforts to green the city were ambitious but failed to stop the encroaching desert. Grass parched out after a single afternoon without water, trees died still girdled in their shipping mesh, and the army of migrant laborers brought to repot sunburned petunias were as unsustainable as the gardens they were hired to plant. At sunset we sat in the shade of dying trees and watched the Indian gardeners dig a shallow grave for a freshly shipped rosebush. "You know those won't root that way," Ma called out.

The men looked up at her, terrified. They'd been gelded by gossip and horror stories of sheikhs' wives who entrapped workers into speaking with them, only to cry rape to their husbands. Ma got up, strode over to them with her cigarette, and squatted down to give them a hand. "You have to dig a *wider* hole," she tried to explain, cigarette still between her teeth. The poor gardeners looked at each other, dropped their tools, and backed away from their plot. They looked about ready to make a run for it. Ma picked the little spade up to show she meant no harm and dug out a hole big enough for the plant. When she'd finished, the two gardeners timidly returned to the job like scavengers who'd been chased off by a lion. The sight of the doomed bushes briefly blooming against the toxic neon of municipal coveralls was sad. "Poor things," Ma commented, though it's difficult to know if she was referring to the plants, the men, or us.

The next Friday afternoon, envoys from Al-Dafira arrived. The day of their arrival Ma had buttoned us into matching pinafores and doused us with her Ysatis eau de toilette, so at the very least we'd make a fragrant impression on them. We were watching from our window when several trucks rumbled up to the entrance of the building. The last of the lineup was a 1979 Suburban, the Bedouin equivalent of the kids' table at a grown-up dinner party. It came bearing a troop of cousins for Dima and me to play with. Ma smoothed our hair and pinched our cheeks to give the illusion of a healthy glow just in time to welcome the women into the house.

When we opened the door, a pack of kids came bursting in and surrounded us. Some of the shy ones hung back near the door, eyes wide and staring at Ma. One of the smaller kids dashed up to her, tagged her leg, and then skittered back off to a safe distance where he could safely observe her. The standoff between Ma and the children broke when she spoke, and although her language was strange, her tone was understood: "I'm not from outer space. I promise." Then, like Ewoks to Leia, the kids gathered around, taking turns touching the cobalt silk of her dress and her thin white hands.

My uncle Mohamed's daughter Alia was closest in age to me, and so we identified one another and immediately fell into cahoots. Despite our language barrier, we communicated in a babelogue of rowdiness. As we got to know one another, the playdate with the other cousins escalated into a riot, and I joined in with the rest in razing the flat. We crowded onto the master bed and leaped for the ceiling, each spring bouncing us higher together. The littlest ones got hurt, tangled in the sheets, or trampled. Somewhere in the savaging of the bedroom we tore the curtains down, we soaked the carpet with the *shadafa* while sword fighting, and I managed to break my own glasses. The liberation of being in a mob didn't last. In the end, I wasn't anonymous enough to escape blame, and Ma snared me out of a skirmish by the nape of my neck and in her deepest, most threatening voice scolded, "You know better than that! What is *wrong* with you!?"

But I was so emancipated by the chaos that I felt no shame. Now that I knew there were two authorities in my life, Ma's rules and the tribe's rules, assimilation equaled rebellion. I bolted with the pack to the door, where we all made off on different bearings, using the stairwell like monkey bars, jumping in the elevators, and scratching graffiti in the wooden doors of neighboring flats. We made it down into the lobby, where the entrance of the building had been converted into a temporary *majlis* by our uncles for the visit. They had rearranged the leather sofas in the waiting area and now sat in a row, tribunal-style, on the black marble floor.

Ma approached the group of men, trailed by the pack of cousins, who emerged from the elevator in a swell and pushed us in close to the men. Dima and I trailed behind her. "*Salam alaikum*," she greeted them in her wide-voweled Arabic.

"*Wa alaikum salam*," the men murmured back. They seemed as apprehensive and even bashful as she did at this meeting.

The men watched silently as she found a perch on the edge of the white leather couch; Dima and I flanked her like cherubs in our fancy dresses and stared back. "Come on, Sophia. Go say hello." Ma pushed me off my seat like she was sending a little boat out into a current.

I went as I'd been bidden to the first man, who offered me his beardy cheek for a kiss, and made the rounds of the room this way, pausing at each person and leaning in for an itchy kiss. Stranger after stranger asked me, "Do you know who I am?" Of course I didn't have a clue and so smiled dimly and nodded "yes," waiting to be passed on to the next man.

Dima, who was still barely toddling, had been watching the whole scene. Normally she wouldn't leave the skirt-clinging radius of Ma, but suddenly and completely on her own she waddled several meters across the carpet toward the row of aged Bedu kings and fell into the arms of a particularly gruff-looking one with an orange beard. "Hi!" she said, and stroked his bright facial hair, fluffing it as though it were a Muppet's fur. Tears welled up in the old man's eyes. "Don' cry. Don' cry," Dima lisped, and patted him on the shoulder the way she would a big gentle dog.

"Dima, you know who that is?" Ma asked.

"Grampa," Dima answered, and the lobby fell silent with surprise.

Despite the fact that he had helped to midwife twelve of his own babies into the world, our grandfather Jabir couldn't seem to figure out how to hold Dima while she carried on chattering to him in English, speaking more to him than she had ever spoken at all.

That night Ma called Puyallup, and we listened in close. "How was company?" Gramma asked.

"It looks like a hurricane hit in here—when they landed I didn't know what was going on. There's nothing left in the house. It's all broken or eaten or just gone." Gramma laughed on the other end, and Ma continued, "I feel like I'm just this white woman living on the outskirts of the reservation raising a couple of kids that belong to the tribe." She paused for Gramma's reply, but if she said anything it was lost in the switchback byways of AT&T's pinched veins. "I keep thinking this is how it must be for astronauts. All cooped up for months on end, not knowing which way is up."

Gramma's voice came through, but it was shredded and unintelligible. Ma rattled the receiver and hit it against her palm like a plugged saltshaker, as though the static could be knocked out. "Mom?" she asked softly. "Are you still there?" When no answer came she kept the phone to her ear for a long time, listening to the dial tone, before she hung up with a sigh.

7

OMICRON² ERIDANI •
THE BROKEN EGGSHELLS • القيض

We remained in a sort of suspended animation while waiting for Baba to come back from the rig. When Baba wasn't with us it was as though time ceased, *we* ceased, and every day in the apartment was just a dream in his periphery. Despite visits from the family, calls to Gramma, and the company of the telescope, Ma was lonely. She tried making friends with a Pakistani guard and a Filipino seamstress and once even lurched at a blue-eyed woman in a *niqab* at the fish market in hopes she might speak English. But she soon found that these people were as foreign as she was in this improbable city. Every week there was a new road, more dust cresting off the construction sites, and higher floors added to the grove of young skyscrapers shooting up around us. It made me dizzy to look up at them from our thirteenth-floor window. I began to fear heights and had dreams of falling: first of plummeting to the ground, then of plunging up into the sky.

Other than trips to the vegetable market and our morning swimming lessons in the tower's pool, we rarely ventured out. Bored senseless like a caged animal, I laid tracks in the carpet by scooting from one end of the window to the other

in an office chair. I imagined myself as an astronaut floating along an observation deck. When I wasn't doing this, I
sprawled on the floor basking in front of the TV until the
carpet had matted into my shape like a nuclear shadow cast
by cathode ray.

Around this time I began to lose my baby teeth, and rip-
ping milk molars out became a hobby of Ma's. Unlike many
other perks of motherhood (the hunting of lice or the pop-
ping of zits, for example), the pulling of teeth allowed her to
assert herself *culturally*. "If there's one thing I'm going to give
my girls it's a mouth full of healthy *American* teeth!"

She developed an array of baroque extraction techniques:
for example, she'd tie an offending tooth to a doorknob, back
me up the appropriate distance, calculate the force required,
and slam the door, leaving me blubbering in a puddle of
drool and tears. When Baba *did* visit, his method was much
more *halal*. He would set me down in front of a cartoon on
TV and vise my neck in his hand so I sat up straight like a
doll in a display stand. This gave me a false sense of security.
Then he'd wait ten or fifteen minutes until Princess Sapphire had fenced off the bad guys, by which time I'd forget I
even had a wiggly tooth. Then, before I could even shout out
or struggle, he'd be holding up a bloody molar for me to see.
"Throw it at the sky and the next one will be better," he told
me, and pushed open the window just a crack for me to toss
the jagged little tooth up into the air and watch it disappear
downward into the construction site below.

The weeklong stretches when Baba did come back were
always highly anticipated. While Ma waited for her driver's

license, Baba's visits were the only times we ever dared to venture far from our isolated little capsule. On one visit about nine months after our arrival, Baba came home from the rig and told Ma to pack.

"But you just got here!" Ma exclaimed.

"And *now* we're going."

"Where? Why?"

"The desert."

Ma stuffed Dima roughly into a onesie, straightening her out with a brisk shake as if she were bagging a pillow. It was just after *maghreb* when we headed out to Baba's rented Land Cruiser. Ma's face was as pale as a porcelain doll with her black *hijab* pulled down tight; Dima dozed against her chest. Baba opened the back of the Land Cruiser and boosted me up inside. As we left the city, I watched the westbound road scroll out under us through the back-door windows—a hypnotic wake of dark concrete pulling me to sleep.

When I woke it was to the idling engine. We had stopped somewhere barren and very dark. I sat up from my nest among the blankets and spare tire. A tall, thin man with a wooden staff came from the night into the red brake lights. As he approached, his eyes darted toward me, though his head stayed still. I ducked back down into the blankets until Baba stepped out and greeted the tall man. They spoke in Arabic. Ma watched suspiciously in the rearview mirror, adjusting her veil nervously.

"*Yalla, Sophie, hawli,*" Baba said, swinging the back door open and reaching to remove me from my nest in the trunk. Dima and I were both wary of the stranger, but Baba reassured us. "He's okay. Go play." We didn't need to be told twice after weeks of playing indoors. We plunged into the fine sand, rolling around like chinchillas in a dust bath. We paused only to prick up our ears at the tense exchange that began between our parents.

"I have to go back to the city for a few hours. I'll be back."

"Why did you bring us out here?"

"Don't worry. He is here to protect you," Baba said, thumbing in the tall man's direction.

Ma's face went long and solemn. "Is this some kind of a joke? Who is he to you? He's a stranger!"

"He is not a stranger, he's Bedu from Sudan."

"I don't care who he is! You're not leaving us here!"

Baba was already perched back in the Land Cruiser, *thobe* stretched taut across his knees, one foot in the car and one foot on the sand.

"You'll be fine."

He shut the door and Ma bared her teeth at Baba through the driver's side window. "Don't!" Ma bellowed, swear words straining behind her clenched teeth.

She was too proud to get hysterical but was mad beyond words, hissing at him as he rolled the window up and drove away.

When the lights of Baba's Land Cruiser disappeared, the stars seemed brighter and the sky more vast. I hung close to Ma as I looked up at the sky, suddenly afraid that without her as an anchor I might fall up. Ma gave the tribesman a wide berth as she stomped back over to the nest, dusted us off, and drew us close. The Sudanese tribesman stared straight ahead, limned in starlight, unmoving. He and the

American farm girl kept eyes askance on each other until a silent truce of mutual distrust was reached and Ma turned her attention safely to us.

"The stars are different here," she said aloud. The light was blue on her pale face, gray on my brown arms. Dima peered sleepily out from under Ma's armpit, where she had burrowed close under the blankets, and Ma rubbed the melted starlight into her cheeks like cream.

"Where did Baba go?" I asked. I kept my head down to avoid the feeling of reverse vertigo I got from the stars.

She drew the points of a constellation in the sand to change the subject. "Can you find the Big Dipper?" I followed her finger while she ran a line between the stars in the sand; this seemed to ease my astrophobia. "Find that one," she ordered.

I tried, but had to squint to avoid feeling dizzy. The sky astigmatized into a bright lacework of light and before I could find the constellation, I was off in a comforting deep sleep.

At some point late in the night, Ma woke me. A meteor shower of rosy gold and silver was passing in the sky. I rubbed my eyes and hugged her close. She squeezed me back. "Sophia, I'm going to have a new baby," she said.

"Will it be like you or like Baba?" was my first question.

"Both of us, of course, honey."

"Will it be a boy?" was my second question.

"We'll see."

"What are the chances?" I asked.

Ma didn't answer as I hugged her belly, enlivened with the idea of a new sibling, and put my eye to the taut, heavy barrel where our new baby lived. I imagined it was a window through which I could see the transparent body of my new brother or sister, backlit in orange and pink. It smiled at me: infinitely wise, alien, imaginary.

"You cannot tell your father. Do you understand?"

I nodded solemnly as she curled me back against her belly. The shadow of the tribesman stood sentry at the top of the dune all night long.

When light broke, the desert was damp, sand still cold with traces of the winter moonlight. The tribesman remained in the same spot and it was only when the camels craned to the east at the sound of an approaching truck that he relaxed his leg and went down to the herd. Baba's Land Cruiser appeared over the dune with a rev that made Ma sit upright from our bundle of blankets, already working her anger up into wrath. By the time Baba pulled the truck up and rolled down his window, all Ma could do was let out a little peep of steam: "That's it!" Baba placed Dima and me in the car without saying a word to her. Ma let him do it, waiting for an apology. But Baba refused eye contact. Ma drew her arm back, first balling it into a fist, and then slapped him.

"God damn you! Goddamnit! How could you leave us? How could you leave us here? How?"

Her voice sounded like it was shredding her throat. But Baba maintained the dead air between them. We drove away from that place without an answer. It would be many months before we got one. I looked back out the rear window of the truck as we drove back toward the city; our guardian, the silent tribesman, stood watch with the camels all around. I waved at him until we were out of sight.

* * *

Almost five months after our night in the desert, Baba still didn't know Ma was expecting, and the rift between them seemed to be growing. When he called from the rig, he started making an effort to speak to Dima and me in Arabic. To Ma, this seemed to be a way to exclude her and a sign of his wavering allegiance. Whenever he called and said *"salam alaikum"* instead of "hello," she hung the phone up on him. There was finality in Ma's movements when she did this, as though she knew it was over before anything was said. She also knew as she harbored the new stranger in her womb that if it were a boy, he would change everything for us, especially within the tribe. Our presence, which for now was at the periphery, would become more central. A boy—a brother—would draw our presence in bolder blood. She wasn't sure what Matar would make of this news. And she didn't tell him until it was too late.

"I felt like if I didn't say it out loud to you it might not be true," she told Baba as he rushed her, miscarrying, to the women's hospital.

Once she was admitted, he was unable to go with her into the "Female Only" maternity ward. Kept at bay by a very aggressive lady security guard, Baba returned to the building, where Dima and I were playing in the lobby under the watch of the Filipino seamstress who ran a shop on our floor.

"You're going camping," he told us.

"But where's Ma?"

"She's sick. She just needs a little rest."

"Can't we stay with her?"

"No."

He packed our clothes and some blankets and that same

night took us to the Saudi border, where our uncle Mohamed was waiting to take us away. We arrived long before morning, and were transferred from Baba's Land Cruiser to the rumbling Suburban *garumba* full of kids, thermoses of coffee, and carpets. Border guards waved us through the checkpoints, preferring not to deal with the rabble. They knew no contraband would be safe in a truck full of feral kids anyway. I recognized Alia and some of our other cousins from the familial summits at our apartment. We fell fast into loud clapping games, and gorged on Vimto and Aladdin chips, bursting off the cracked cement of Salwa Road and into the unpaved Jafoorah Desert—a track of djinn-haunted land no one dared cross unless they started in the morning and could ensure making it across by dusk.

As soon as we went off road we hit a dip. All of us piled in the back hovered over the rusted-out floor of the trunk. Just as the tires hit the ground and we hit our heads, the back doors of the Suburban swung open wide like French doors in a thunderstorm. Dima and I clung to each other, but it didn't seem to bother the other kids at all. Uncle Mohamed drove like a daredevil; he went into a sort of Zen trance, matching gears and speed to the individual personality of each erg. We broke the top of an ordinary-looking dune to find our camp hidden behind it. Consisting of ten large "hair-houses," or tents woven out of wiry black goat fur, they were so black against the white land that the opening of each looked as though it were the entrance to a deep cave.

A small Nissan pickup appeared beside us on the top of the dune. The bed of the truck was full of scraggly firewood and at the wheel was our aunt Falak, her twin brother, Faraj, in the passenger seat. She flashed the lights at Uncle Mohamed and guided us down the almost vertical slope into the camp. Falak and Faraj were only about fourteen years old then. I remember being impressed with the two as they stepped out of the truck and came to greet us. Falak wore a fluorescent pink and yellow *jalabiya*, with a black *hijab* tied loosely around her head that had fallen off the back like a hoodie. Our uncle Faraj wore a *thobe*, and his *gutra* covered his face. Falak put me at ease and Faraj scooped Dima up to tickle her. Despite their youth they were both strangely grown up, as was the case with many of the older boys and girls. Once they had passed the rabble-age (from toddling to about ten), they helped take care of the young stragglers like us.

Falak led Dima and me to a big tent at the edge of the camp. This was the collective storage tent where everyone piled their bedding during the day. The ground was covered with foam bed pads all sewn into psychedelic floral prints; the edges were stacked with cushions, forming a fortress that was filled with mounded multicolored quilts. Dima and I fell into the soft quilts and fell into a deep sleep from exhaustion, confusion, and a little bit of fear at being so far from our parents.

When I woke it was dark outside. "I have to pee," I whined to the darkness. Nothing. "Wake up!" I prodded at Dima. But her wheezy little snores were all I got. The tent had been emptied of all the bedding by now, but for the blanket we were bundled in together. I rose and peeked out the flap at the other areas of the tent cluster. The stars and moon were bright like a black light and made the white sand glow ultraviolet. I steered clear of the shadows and snuck around the back of the camp facing up against a dune and fashioned a little dugout for myself. All around was silence, and the stars were even brighter than they had been the night in the desert with the tribesman. The only light came from one of the open tent flaps, and the silence was suddenly broken by the wail of a baby.

I hopped away from my puddle in the sand and walked toward the light. A flap of black wool flickered in the breeze, and a baby bawled from inside. I remembered Ma and wondered if she and our baby brother were feeling better yet. I thought maybe I should go back to Dima, and then I realized I didn't know which of the identical black wool tents I'd left her in. The baby cried again, and now I could make out a gas lantern hanging on the main post in the middle; underneath this I saw the figure of an old woman. She drew me in like a tractor beam, and I startled when I got close enough to see that she was watching me. Her body was wide, and she sat flat with legs akimbo. Her *jalabiya* was dark calico, her gray braids were red with henna, a black *berga* covered her face, and her underwear was long, with a ringlet of embroidered starbursts circling her ankles.

I hung shyly at the door. "Do you know who I am?" she asked.

Although I never knew the answer when anyone else asked me this question, somehow I *did* know this was my grandmother, Umi Safya, my Arabic namesake. But I was too terrified to answer her for fear I'd be wrong. She lifted the corner of her *berga* and offered her smooth cheek for me to kiss, then held me by the shoulders and sat me down roughly beside her. She grasped a loom between her toes, a stick knotted with the ends of rough camel-hair yarn she was weaving into some kind of rope.

"How's your mama?" she asked and offered me a piece of sour, salty cheese. It was about the size, shape, and consistency of a sand dollar, and had the indents of her fingers in it like a fork across our other grandmother's peanut-butter cookies. "Did you come to see your brother?"

I didn't understand what she meant. Ma and my little brother were in Doha. How could they be here? And if they were *here*, why hadn't anyone told us?

"Ey! The little stranger came to see her brother," Umi said to someone I hadn't noticed in the corner of the tent. She directed me with a rough push toward the shadows and went back to braiding her sling of yarn into rope.

The woman's body in the corner was a sea of black but for the white island of a boob, spilling over the neckline of her *jalabiya* and into the mouth of a little baby. "Come here." She beckoned to me. Her voice came harsh through her veil. "His name is Badr," she told me. I looked down at the tiny brown baby suckling at her black areola.

"Badr," I repeated dumbly, still puzzling over why Umi had called him my brother.

"It means full moon."

She then propped him against her knee, his legs akimbo on a pile of blankets like a helpless specimen, so I could get a good look at him. I studied this little human she was presenting to me. His tiny fingers balled up and pawed at the air like a turtle on its back, and his tears were stained black by the kohl powder around his eyes. He had a thick black tuft of hair waving straight up from his head like Astro Boy. His snot glistened, mixed with tears in the dim light, and when I touched him his face clenched in displeasure and he began howling again.

"Can't you see he needs winding?" Umi Safya commented from the sidelines.

"Take him to your grandmother," the woman ordered.

He blinked up at me with his wet eyes. I didn't understand who this little person was to me. *How* he could be my brother? I held him at the armpits, unsure what to do with him, and carefully picked my way through the colorful tangle of blankets on the ground. He had a scrap of fabric filled with cardamom and other spices called a *khomra*. It was effective at warding off bad spirits, less so at preventing gas. Umi Safya slung Badr's tiny body over her knee as casually and roughly as picking a kitten out of the basket by its nape. Then, patting him in rhythm with the rocking of her knee, she calmed his tears by howling at him in a mock baby's cry: "*Lebaay! Lebaay!*" until he fell silent and then asleep.

Back in Doha, Ma was alone in the women's hospital while Baba was trying to bribe his way in to see her. But by the next morning she had lost my brother, propelling his little body from hers. He never made it to oxygen, fading as he passed through the birth canal like an asteroid burning up on entry into the atmosphere. When she woke a few hours later, all she wanted was a smoke. She struggled up, rummaged through her purse, shuffled to the bathroom, and lit a cigarette. She was dizzy and when she looked down she found she was also bleeding. The blood didn't surprise her—she had just had a miscarriage. However, when she fell to the floor in a faint and was found curled around the toilet in her green hospital gown, cigarette doused in a pool of her own blood, the nurses assumed the worst. A delegation of doctors came from all points of the hospital: Syrians, Indians, Russians.

When Ma awoke her legs were pushed up, knees-to-ears, and they were examining her. "Get off! Leave me alone! Where is my husband?"

Ignoring her, the doctors came to a unanimous guess: "She is bleeding internally!"

Ma popped the IV out of her arm and tried to get out of the bed, screaming for help.

"Perhaps we ought to put the patient under mental observation," suggested one of the doctors.

But nothing makes a person crazier than being told she is crazy. They had to get six nurses to hold Ma down until the tranquilizers kicked in, her intensity diluting as the sedatives entered her bloodstream. She was still awake when they rolled her into an operating theater for the unexplained "emergency operation." She described it later as a mad scientist's lab. Despite the fact that her own husband couldn't pass through the wards, she found that men were huddled all around her, most in surgical masks but some in suits. They covered her eyes and that was the last thing she remembered until her reentry into the outer rings of consciousness, brought painfully into focus by an intense burning sensation spreading up her arm. She cast around, wanting to scream at the masked men. But they were gone, and now only Matar sat by her side while a nurse squeezed a big bag of blood into her veins.

A few days later Dima and I returned from the desert.

Ma was still in the hospital. She was whiter than usual, and she seemed to be suspended in a web of transparent tubes. Her eyes fluttered open, and she patted a patch of the white sheet for us to climb up on. I scrambled up ahead of Dima, my purple dress shedding sand all over the bed.

"You girls are filthy. Where have they been?" she asked.

"With their family," Baba answered for us, and pulled up a rolling office chair alongside the bed.

"Oh, that's nice. What did you kittens get up to?"

I launched into a rapid-fire rundown of our adventures, dumping the specimens I had kept from our travels onto her blanket. I displayed a snakeskin, a sand rose, a shiny chip wrapper, and the dry goat poop and white pebbles for sand tic-tac-toe to illustrate. I was reveling on the bed in my stash of treasures when I excitedly added, "Oh, and guess what? I met our little brother!"

Baba tensed, and Ma pulled herself up gingerly into a sitting position. "Oh, kitten. I'm so sorry." I didn't understand the commiseration as she pulled me to her, planting a long kiss on the part of my matted braids. "I need to tell you something. There's not going to be any little brother."

"Why? Where's he gone?"

"Just gone."

I didn't protest, comforted by being back in Ma's arms. But as she rocked Dima and me back and forth in the cradle of her IV tubes, I saw a shadow darken Baba's face, a tiny hint at the shattering disaster about to make deep impact on our little world.

8

DELTA ARIETIS •
THE LITTLE BELLY • بطين

Ma's pale skin showed the blotchy red rash of the infestation first. The burrowing mites weren't as evident on our darker skin until the pruritus left us squirming, rubbing our backs against the spiny Astroturf alongside the building's swimming pool. The pregnant females had burrowed under our skin and let loose with trails of their microscopic eggs.

"This looks like scabies," Ma said, holding a magnifying glass up to her skin and then back down into her circa-1950 reference book of children's maladies. "Either you girls got them in the desert or I picked them up in the hospital," she concluded.

The doctor gave us a prescription salve and we underwent a routine quarantine in our little flat in the big city like astronauts returning to earth. He instructed Ma to boil all fabrics, stuffed animals in particular. So Dima and I sat by in the kitchen letting the hot vapors scald our cheeks while we whimpered in protest as our stuffed animals were plopped into the boiling cauldron like plush lobsters.

The scabies rash was still visible the week Baba was due for his land leave from the rig. We hadn't seen him since

Ma had come home from the hospital, and she did her best to make us presentable, wrestling us into our best dresses and ruffled socks. She seemed nervy that morning as she trammeled me by my ponytail and dragged the brush down through the tangled mess.

"You're killing me!" I howled, certain I was *actually* dying from the pain.

"It hurts to be beautiful." She punctuated the truism with a pitiless yank.

"Cut it off!" I shrilled.

Unsympathetic, Ma finished ruthlessly plowing my hair into rows.

"Don't talk like that, most girls would die to have nice thick hair like yours. Besides, your Baba wants his girls to have long hair."

She finished banding me into the braid and I stationed myself as far away from her brush as possible at the window to sulk. That afternoon the sun seemed to hover at half-mast forever as I pressed my tear-stained cheeks against the glass. Construction had just begun on the office tower across from us when we arrived in Doha, and we had watched its rebar and cement hatch from the ground like crocuses in the spring. Now it had almost matched the height of our own building. I looked across at it, my lips suctioned against the glass of the window, watching dimly, like a goldfish.

The first thing I noticed was the shade cast over the sun by a sudden plume of dust. Then our whole building wavered like a stack of books, and Ma dragged us under the dining room table in case we went down too. After the quake had settled, Ma crawled to the window and looked out. "Oh, no," she started repeating to herself. "Oh, no!" and held Dima and me back from looking. The entire tower that had been under construction kitty-corner to us had collapsed on itself. Later we learned that the workers had accidentally walled a bulldozer into the building and tried to drive it through the unreinforced lobby doors to get it out. I morbidly craned the telescope down from its usual coordinates and scanned the mess, looking for blood or guts or any color at all in the mealy gray rubble. But all I spied from my perch before Ma pulled me away from the telescope were the remnants of a red-checkered *gutra*.

By the time Baba finally arrived that afternoon, the ambulances had come and gone. The construction accident had shaken Ma. It seemed like a bad omen of things to come. As Baba entered, she held back in the living room like a dog straining at its leash. He was uncharacteristically somber. He kissed me without a word and didn't seem to notice the scabies rash or the fishbone braids I'd suffered for. Ma lifted Dima from the floor and put her to bed, then she led me into the bedroom and bundled me in. I pouted and threw the covers off.

"Stay down," she warned, and went back out to the living room.

But the twang of the TV turning on drew me out from the covers. I snuck to the open bedroom door and peered out to where my parents sat. Baba slouched on the floor cushions, flicking through the channels on the TV. All I could see of Ma was the ripple of gold hair draped down her back. I went back to bed and fell asleep to the comforting sound of television fuzz. Then at some point in the night Ma came back into our room, silhouetted in the darkened hall. I knew something was different but couldn't recognize what. Shock seeps through in the strangest ways. A tight staccato of realizations hit me, and I saw her holding fistfuls of her own long, blond hair, like she'd scalped Rapunzel. She crawled into the bed with us and lay still.

"What's the matter?" I asked, frightened. Her silence seemed dangerous, a volatile kind of hush.

But she was silent, just staring in the darkness. Then Baba came into the doorway; Ma hurled the fistful of hair at him. He caught it out of the air and curled it around his hand like a bandage. "What you want me to do?"

He seemed to shrink in the doorway, but he was really just walking away. The apartment door slammed behind him and Ma lay down in a fetal position between Dima and me. "Your baba has another wife," she sobbed. I remembered the breastfeeding woman in the desert. We really did have a little brother after all.

Most people who hear the following part of the story think our father was being cruel. But in reality, he was just clueless. He brought his *other* wife, Flu, with him the next day. She was indeed the woman I'd met in the desert, and she carried our little brother, Badr, with her. Baba announced that Flu would be staying with us and moved her suitcase into one of the bedrooms. He said he was worried about Ma being here all alone, that Flu could help her around the house and take care of us. "She'll teach the girls Arabic," he offered. But Ma was too shocked at his utopian delusions to answer.

"You're crazy if you think I'm going to live like some fucking hippie on a commune!" she shouted and corralled Baba into the kitchen, where she slammed the door. Meanwhile, Dima and I watched Flu. Baba's big secret sat in one of the unused bedrooms, a specter in black *berga*, nursing Badr silently on the bare mattress. Down the hall we could hear Ma crying through the walls of the kitchen. Baba went through a long explanation detailing *his* story: Flu was his cousin from Saudi, and his brother Mohamed had convinced him to marry her because she needed help. She lived on the outskirts of a little town in a shack with her sisters and widowed mother. All of them had ended up becoming second wives because they were so poor. She and Badr lived there still in her mother's un-air-conditioned, running water–less hut while he was on the rig.

"You said yourself the flat was big enough for two families!"

"I can't *believe* you twist my words in my mouth!" Ma blew the door open and stomped to where we waited near Flu. Ma grabbed Badr from Flu and lifted him like she was weighing a piece of meat. "How old? Six months?" she barked at Flu. She calculated the approximate time of our castaway night in the desert with the tribesman, and then put two and two together. She pointed at Flu and the baby without looking at them. "So *that* is why you left us in the desert that night? Don't lie."

Baba went into the bathroom and locked himself in. Ma went to sit in the living room. Flu followed and sat across from her on the swiveling office chair. Ma ordered us to her. "Come 'ere, girls." She lit a cigarette (which she *never* did indoors) and drew us to her, creating a united front against the *other* female encroaching on her territory. Sweaty metal bangles slid up and down Flu's hairless arm while she waved away the thick Marlboro smoke Ma was blowing in her direction.

Dima hid behind the armchair, peeking out at the heavily perfumed woman. No sound from Baba in the bathroom. Flu adjusted her *berga* with a tug, like an old man pulling his beard. Ma sat stiffly in her armchair, her expression shifting from devastation to hysteria to hatred. She offered Flu a crystal cup of tea, a plate of wilted grapes, a smoke. Flu made a clicking noise of no from under her veil each time. Not to be refused, Ma pushed me forward.

Flu took my hand in hers. I looked at Ma for approval, but she was back to watching the bathroom door and wasn't listening anymore.

Flu swept me up and forced my locked knees until I was sitting on her lap. I struggled in her grip; the coarse embroidery on her *jalabiya* made my rash itch even more. Still no sound came from the bathroom. What would be the right etiquette for this situation? An all-out brawl probably would not have been frowned upon. They could have scratched each other's eyes out, throttled, beat, maimed, or—as Al-Dafira tradition goes for the settlement of such disputes—disemboweled each other. Instead they sat at the table while the tea leaves sank and listened together for the toilet to flush.

What seemed like an hour passed before Baba emerged, sheepish, giving a fearful look to Ma and a pitiful one to Flu. This was my chance to get away. I wriggled off Flu's lap, relieved of shield-duty protecting her from Ma's evil eye. Flu showily kissed my forehead before Baba took her back into the bedroom where Badr was asleep. Ma said nothing as the sun set into night. No sound came from the bedroom. She fixed us a dinner of canned tuna and pocket bread, plotting all the while what to do. In the end, the silence coming from the room drove her to germ warfare.

After she'd washed us up for bed, Ma gave me a kiss on my prickly-rashed forehead. "I want you to go sleep in the room with Baba," she said, and opening the door a crack, she nudged me into the dark room. "I'm sorry, kitten," she whispered in my ear.

I didn't know what she was sorry about and felt my way toward the bed, where I could barely make out two dark heaps under the sheet. "Baba?" I asked of the dark figure in the bed. No sound came from the heap. I crawled up, doing Ma's bidding like a smallpox-infected blanket sent straight to Chief Pontiac. Baba pulled me up and nestled me in between him and Flu. Badr squirmed beside me. I could see his puckered lips suckling at the air, dreaming, as I imagine babies do, of big tits in the sky. Flu was snoring steadily, every third breath ending in a snort. I concentrated on the rhythm until I too fell into sleep, waking only occasionally to scratch.

The next morning Ma dressed in the blue morning-glory outfit she had bought to meet our family. The monochrome was broken only by the dots of pink rouge on her cheeks, efforts at a healthy glow only drawing attention to how weak and tired she actually looked. After the surgical nightmare she had become practically translucent, and I had become obsessed with tracing the topography of her blue veins through her skin. Dima was spacing out in front of the living room window chewing a cocktail sausage. Ma's recovery meant we'd been living off canned food, triangle cheese, and juice boxes for weeks. Ma had packed the suitcase with our few possessions that had *not* been gifts from Baba. Depending on his movements this morning she would make an executive decision about our future as a family unit. By the time we left the apartment, the light in the window was tinted with an orange, martian glow. A sandstorm was approaching. Baba stepped into the hall just as we left and watched us get into the elevator. They said nothing to each other and within minutes Ma, Dima, and I were in a cab driving into the darkening storm.

"How will Baba know where we are?" I whined from the backseat.

"He'll know," Ma said in her emergency voice, the deep one that warned us not to argue.

Visibility was so low on the roads that the cabdriver had to inch forward as we passed into the eerie billows of the sandstorm and finally came to the corniche where the apex of the Sheraton Hotel rose over the dashboard. The massive ziggurat of the Sheraton was even more impressive to me now than it had been in Baba's video. It squatted low on its reclaimed pilings like a broken-down spaceship caught in the earth's enchantment. We passed through a series of automatic doors, each sealing us off further from the storm—closer to sanctuary, hermetically sealed from the confusion of our culture and our family. Entering it was like stepping into a gigantic, glamorous terrarium from the future. The soft hiss of chlorinated spray misted from tiled fountains, teacups clinked on their saucers, the concierge smiled.

As long as we stayed inside this temple to unreality and out of the sandstorm, we could suspend belief and forget the fact that our father had married another woman and that she had been the one to birth a brother. Ma checked us in under a false name and, having no money, gave them our passports as collateral at the desk. Someone would have to bail us out of the hotel if we were ever going to leave. A bellhop led us into the elevators. The doors were brass, the ceiling mirrored with triangles of colored glass. A full view of the patterned fountains sprawled below us as the elevator rose and a double-breast of buttons glowed out of the side panel.

The doors opened, we stepped out to a landing, and he led us to our room. The sandstorm gave a day-for-night quality to our view. All hours seemed the same. There's no way for me to know the duration of our stay; it was probably only days, but it seemed to me like a long time. Ma didn't want us to draw attention by playing outside in the halls or lobby, so she tried to amuse us by making floppy origami cranes out of napkins and reading aloud from the hotel pamphlets on the bedside table. "Listen to this, girls!" she'd begin enthusiastically before sharing some unimpressive piece of trivia. "The American astronaut Alan Shepard was the first person to check in here!"

It was in the liminal hours of what might have been early morning when a soft knock came at our door. Ma opened the door to a black specter. It was Flu. Baba had found us and sent her to apologize.

"*Ecomme. Dawen,*" she said through her *berga.*

"I'm not gonna calm *dawen.*" Ma mocked her. She was about to slam the door, but Flu intercepted it, hennaed fingers in the doorjamb.

"Come. Down." This time she enunciated. "Matar. Down." She pointed downward toward the lobby. Ma let go and released Flu's hand.

"Kittens, I'll be right back," Ma said, and left with Flu.

I turned to Dima, who had fashioned a cushion-throne for herself at the head of the bed, remote control in hand. We blinked at each other. Dima turned back to the TV. I quietly opened the door and snuck into the hallway. It was empty, and in the near distance I heard the chime of the elevator: aural catnip.

Shuffling down the hall, I pressed my ear to the wall and listened to the hum of invisible machines running the mother ship of the building. I made it to the elevator, where I was conducted safely down the warren of ranked halls and stairwells, descending into the lobby. The cobalt of my mother's *hijab* glinted from under the filigree of a café gazebo. She was smoking and sitting across a table from Baba and Flu.

I ducked low under the window rail so she wouldn't see me. Ma gesticulated at them with her cigarette, bartering for our status as his first family. Her intensity had faded since our first day in the building, but her anger hadn't. She gazed over Baba's shoulder at the player-less piano and dragged long on her cigarette. Just as I landed at L, Ma turned and stared directly at me like an owl spying a mouse. I pressed the highest button I could reach as she stood and mouthed my name.

I blanched and then for some reason waved, knowing I was going to get into trouble for leaving the room anyway.

The button I had pressed turned out to lead onto a winding hallway lined with tarnished brassy mirrors. The lights were dimmed, but the same automated rendition of "Bright Eyes" dusted down from the ceiling speakers. Following the hallway to its mouth I came to an empty restaurant, also brass, with a great Fibonacci-sequenced chandelier hanging over the tables. A panoramic floor-to-ceiling view of the sandstorm (now all pink and copper) rimmed the room, something between the grandeur and the emptiness belted together to mute the space, and I stood stunned and disoriented by the mirrors and windows and the wind.

Somewhere beyond one of the mirror panes I heard the scraping of silver on a plate. One seam in the mirror was darker and wider than the others. I pushed it a little and it slid open. This was the private wing of the restaurant. I peeked in, stepped through, and came up behind a row of potted palm trees lining the entrance of a private elevator flanked by two silver oryx. Kids my age were bickering, and I leaned in between the fronds to see an Indian maid standing at the sideboard near a triangulated bay window; behind him hints of coast were visible every few seconds through the continuing storm. A man with a mustache sat at the head of the table, *thobe* crisp and white, *gutra* folded up in the aggressive "cobra" style of the time. To his right sat a fair woman in a silk dress ruched at the neck. To his left sat a distinctly Arab woman with long black hair hanging in a braid over the back of her chair. The adults ate in silence while two sets of children all around the same age tossed saltine crackers like *shuriken* at one another under the table. The two boys to the right of the table had light brown hair like the woman in the stylish silk dress. The three to the right were heavier-set and wearing *thobes*. All five were vying for the man's attention.

Here, in the uppermost cockpit of the Sheraton, was the dream my father imagined for himself: an alternate reality where his wives and children clustered around him on a Friday morning. He wasn't being cruel when he brought Flu to stay with us; he was trying (unsuccessfully) to assume a lifestyle far beyond his means.

I felt Ma's presence behind me before she made herself known. I didn't turn around. I knew she was watching the scene too, making the same assumptions I was about the rich family in the VIP room. Grasping my shoulder, she held tight at first, and then I felt the urgency, the desperation, the anger, and the static all zap out of her in a resigned understanding. When my mother and I finally backed out through the mirrored secret door, my father was waiting for us. Flu stood near the corridor with Dima hitched up in her arms. Ma patted me toward Baba. "It's okay, kitten. We're not angry anymore."

When day broke we went early to the airport in Doha, where we had reunited with Baba more than a year earlier. Baba entered and, as was his way, found us without looking for us. For the first time he and Ma seemed to understand each other; the naivety of a decade spent coming together and then drifting apart was scrubbed away. All that was left were his obligations and her expectations. He held Dima and me close, taking off his *gutra* to give us a good squeeze before lifting us around our bellies like a pair of goat kids and handing us over to Ma.

"*Ma'a salama*, Matar," she said, with her learned accent skipping and slurring the phrase.

He nodded and kissed her forehead in the same gesture of respect he would have given his mother. And like his father at the Doha airport all that time ago, he said a prayer: "*Estowda'a Allah al lethi la yethia'a wada'ai.*"

Once we were on the plane, Ma removed her *hijab*. Dima and I gaped; it was like seeing your mother strip down nude in public. She unclipped the silk triangle from her chin and stuck the safety pin into the foam of our seat. Even with the hack job she'd done cutting her hair, in the dismal light of the cabin it was bright yellow blond. She folded the *hijab* up and slipped it into her seat pocket with the barf bag and escape instructions. Latched into my window seat, I pressed my forehead to the double-paned glass, wishing it would open like the skin of a soap bubble and let me fall back to Baba. Red satellites blinked above, orange city grids below, as we passed into the blackness of the Empty Quarter. Yellow and blue oil flares blossomed up from the night desert, and that was the last I saw of *that* home for a long time.

9

GAMMA ANDROMEDAE •
HUG THE GROUND • عناق الأرض

Little had changed on the farm since we'd left, although the housing developments were getting bigger and the freeway was a lot busier. Ma's trusty Scirocco squatted over an oil pool in the carport where she had left it, gold paint flaking away to reveal rust patches on the hood and sides. It was berry season and U-pickers had come out to the fields, loading up flats of raspberries and hauling them away. I observed Gramma closely in her daily activities and compared her with our other grandmother, Umi Safya. They didn't seem so different. One wore a muumuu from Honolulu and the other a *jalabiya* from Al-Hassa. They both bent the same way at the waist when they rooted along the ground for weeds or truffles. Both of them wore rings that were too tight for their fingers, and both of them knitted for fun.

I'd been too young when we left to have much conscious memory of the place, but the feeling of familiarity welled up through subtler sensations: for example, the way the soggy blades of grass squelched under my feet, the sonic boom of Fighter Falcons echoing off Mount Rainier, the smell of Gramma's cold cream. Then there was muscle memory.

Out in the desert I'd bounded around with my heels to the ground; here I skidded and slipped on the grass if I did that. Even Dima took ginger steps walking on the lawn. "You making a moon landing there, kid?" Gramma teased from the sidelines as Dima picked her way carefully across the garden.

By July Baba's cologne had faded from our clothes and we were settled into American life. But American life was not synonymous with a freer life. Ma was so fearful of strangers that we were effectively under house arrest. Strangers were understood to mean *men*, who were *all* wolves to Ma, regardless of whether they were senile veterans or serial killers. "The more harmless they look, the more dangerous they are," she warned us. I'd press my face up against the windows like I used to in apartment 1303. Whenever a jet flew over from McChord Air Force base I could feel its vibrations in my skull and wished I could go for a ride back to Doha. If I did leave the house, I was to be chaperoned by Gramma's dog, Alf, and had to promise never to speak to any strangers. So it was that one stir-crazy afternoon, Alf and I were racing each other through the field. We made it up the quarter-mile stretch to the cul-de-sac and were running back up to the house when I saw a stranger smoking on the steps of the front porch. He was wearing an army-surplus jacket over grease-smeared flannel and army boots. He had a mustache and longish hair and dark skin just like Baba. Like a fish tricked by a fly-looking lure, I went for him and inexplicably brayed, "Hi . . . *Dad*!"

I clapped my hand over my mouth. It had come out so loud; the word "Dad" echoed off the mountainside, taunting

me. I wanted to throw up right after I said it. I didn't even
know why I'd done it. The stranger paused in the drag off his
cigarette and squinted long and thin at me. I wanted to disappear, dig a hole to Doha and then never come back again.
The stranger knocked Alf's head away and stood up to step
out his smoke. I watched him as he disappeared through the
fields and down the path that led to the river. Ma pulled in
just as he passed beyond the property line. She slammed
the car door, made a few steps as if she would go after him,
and then turned and grabbed me by my shoulders, "Did that
man try to talk to you?"

"Nope," I answered, hoping she hadn't heard the terrible
echo of my mistake.

Shortly after the "Dad" incident with the stranger, Ma
started nighttime vocational school. This was the early '90s
near Seattle, so mastering C++, Pascal, and other computer
languages seemed like a *very* viable skill to develop. This
meant she was gone every night until eleven, which also
meant Gramma, Dima, and I were left alone in the house.
This not only made her feel guilty, in typical single-mother
fashion, but made her become deeply paranoid. After my
encounter with the stranger on the porch steps, she saw the
specter of pedophiles and burglars and child abductors everywhere, and fair enough—the farmhouse was isolated at
the end of a private road in the middle of several high-traffic
routes for the homeless and hobos. The river running south
of us had overgrown orchards where the trunks were marked
up with the obscure codes and warnings for the transients
who passed through. The highway to the north was a regular
route for hitchhikers. The trailer park to our east, with its

aluminum-sided trailers of daiquiri- and sherbet-colors, was mostly full of senior citizens—but Ma's guard remained up, whether a man was eighteen or eighty.

One evening toward the end of the summer, we were watching an episode of *Unsolved Mysteries* about Sasquatch in Gramma's room when there was a yelp and crash against the front screen. It was Alf letting out an odd tremolo, a high-pitched cross between a whimper and a scream. Another smash! In seconds I was crawling out into the dark of the living room. As my eyes adjusted to the dark I saw Ma standing in the middle of the front parlor with the shotgun.

"Gale—what the hell's going on out there?" Gramma yelled.

"I don't know," Ma hissed back over her shoulder in our direction, then turned to the door. "Go wake your dad up, boys!" she yelled for the attacker's benefit.

"But he's not here!" I squeaked, hopping from foot to foot in a panic.

"Not really!" she hissed back. "So they think we've got a man in here with us."

Another crash against the screen. She flinched and backed up a pace. It was so blindingly black outside.

"I've got a twelve-gauge Remington Model Eleven semi-automatic shotgun, pal, and you better believe I'll use it!" she bellowed.

The barrel was so long it looked like a broom handle from where I was. Seeing Ma with the huge weapon was almost as distressing as the idea that one of the many male specters she had conjured up for us was now *really* outside trying to get in.

"Sophia. The phones," she said without taking her eyes off the door. I tried pulling the phone out to her but the cord was too short. "Stay back, stay back," she ordered me. "Leave the phone on the floor and back up." She was afraid I'd get too close to the gun, like in a hostage-trade situation.

She kept the gun trained on the door and inched back to where I'd placed the phone on the floor. She dialed 911 just as Alf let out another horrible cry. "Yes, hello! Someone is trying to break into our house." There was a kick at the door. We all jumped. "Yes, it has five shells and one in the chamber," Ma answered. "Myself and my mother and my children."

The drapes were starting to shake now, the screen door had been broken through, and now the inner door's handle started to jiggle. A flashlight beam was shining through the keyhole, and, eerily, we could see no shadow.

Ma addressed me—"Sophie! Take Gramma and Dima into the bedroom and hide"—before turning and issuing a threat in the direction of the door: "The sheriff's on the way, buddy!"

She sat in the living room in wait in a rocking chair, listening to the creaking of the busted screen door, shotgun up on her knee and the phone stretched as close as she could get it. She continued her loud bluff for the intruder. "The good thing about a shotgun is you can get 'em at close range!" But the sounds outside had stopped.

It had all lasted only about ten minutes, though it seemed as if it had been an hour when the phone rang. It was the operator: "Put the gun away, ma'am. The sheriff's outside now."

Ma unloaded the Remington and put it away, opened the front drapes, and switched on the lights. The screen door was ripped to shreds; Alf was shaking, and as soon as the door opened he bolted inside, claws clacking on linoleum as he came scuttling back to where we were hidden. Ma went with the sheriff and his men to make double-sure whoever it was was good and gone. She led them around the side of the house where their spotlights shone into our bedroom, casting a thick circular light on the curtains like the eye of a giant squid. They checked the shed and all the hiding places Ma could think of and followed the berry tines all the way down to the river, but found nothing.

That night Ma called Baba for the first time since we had left. His voice was deeper than I remembered, more like the voice of a stranger. He was at Umi Safya's crowded house; it was Friday there and the room sounded warm and festive. Bright sounds of children crying and women bantering came over the line, in sharp contrast to the dark silence of our living room. As we listened, I yearned for the safety that came in those numbers. Of how secure I had felt when I was with the larger pack. Only then did I realize I might be missing that other home, only then did the farm start to feel lonely.

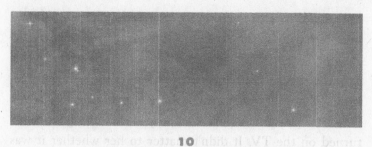

10
EPSILON ORIONIS •
THE STRING OF PEARLS • النّظم

The portrait of Baba still looked straight at me from the man-
telpiece. No matter where I moved, from the davenport to
the TV to the hearth, he was watching me. The news at the
time was preoccupied with another omnipresent face with
a mustache—Saddam. Every weeknight we sat together in
the living room with Gramma and watched the five o'clock
news, mostly illustrated with stock footage of fighter jets and
green night-vision desert. Whenever a map of the Gulf came
on-screen, it had topographical features rather than political borders. Despite being a distinctive part of the Arabian
Peninsula's geography, Qatar was often left off the map alto-
gether, so Dima and I would race to mark it on the television
with a little extension of Silly Putty, which would stick to
the screen throughout the broadcast like a saggy pink blem-
ish on the anchor's face. The absence of borders on the maps
made everything seem extra close together, and the fact that
our family was there somewhere between the cartoon barrel
of the tank gun and the cyan blue of the "Persian" sea was
hard to comprehend.

Feeling it was her civic duty to correct the local news,

Ma called in to the station to ensure they knew it should
be referred to as the Arabian Gulf. And yet the news anchor persisted in calling that little nubbin of water on his
map the Persian Gulf. However, he wasn't the only one who
kept stubbornly to his mistakes. "Is old Hoodam Sudain at
it again?" Gramma would say apropos of nothing when we
turned on the TV. It didn't matter to her whether it was
"Hoodam" instead of Saddam, "AbiDabbi" instead of Abu
Dhabi, or "old man Jibber Jabber" instead of our grandfather
Jabir.

We all watched together as the news anchor forecasted
the Iraqi army's movements like a weatherman, moving little
tank icons around the cartoonish map like thunderclouds.
Despite the fact that we lived only a few miles from the
U.S. Air Force base and were used to seeing huge hawk-like
Stealth bombers and strange lights filling the sky on summer
nights, the scenes of air raids alarmed Ma. She kept in close
contact with Baba on the phone during that time, calling
him to overreact every time they showed laser-light footage of air raids more than a thousand kilometers away. He
always knew the appropriate reaction, to shrug them off as
blithely as if they were scattered showers.

Before school started, Ma got a new job at a software
company called Helden Systems. Dima and I spent those
first days on our own sneaking all the things we'd never been
allowed to watch: the loving, wise fathers on shows like *The
Cosby Show* and *Full House* made our own home feel empty,
whereas Carl Sagan in his polystyrene cockpit had always
filled us with wonder. Ma didn't want us to watch those
shows for a reason; they gave us ideas about what we might

be missing. We did our best not to voice our dissatisfaction. Whenever she came home proudly bearing reams of dot-matrix printer paper and dry-erase markers salvaged from a Dumpster at work for us to play with, we pretended to be thrilled, wishing all along Baba would come to visit and take us to Toys "R" Us to buy My Little Ponies. Ma did her best to entertain us with cheaper pursuits like making cornstarch "moon mud," and took time away from programming for some flow-chart fun, teaching us how to make process diagrams.

"You start with a problem and you end with a solution. So you link the question and the answer through steps you represent with these little boxes."

She waggled the transparent stencil at me. "Go ahead. Just think of a problem," she coaxed. "And answer it."

Then she swiveled back to her black DOS screen.

I looked down at the disordered chaos I had been scribbling, the beginnings of a house with trapezoid windows. The only problem I could think of to fix was our family. So I began plotting out my lineage, taping two pieces of computer paper to the kitchen wall beside each other. Starting with two end points—triangles representing Dima and me—I worked up. The problem burst backward from the fix. Men were represented by parallelograms, women by ovals, and kids by diamonds. I traced red lines between men and women who were married and stenciled blue lightning bolts off these to link kids to their parents. The paternal side of the chart quickly filled up and refused to fit onto the page neatly like my mother's family. On my fifth try I became so frustrated by the lack of symmetry caused by multiple wives that I wadded both sides up and stuffed them and the flow-chart stencil into the garbage, and returned to my aimless doodling.

After she received her certification, Ma's continuing obsession with ensuring we had American teeth led her to take a temp job at an orthodontist's office over a higher-paying entry-level position at Boeing. She was relieved to finally be able to afford to get us into braces and head-gear. "This is for your own good. You want the other kids to make fun of your buckteeth?" But Ma's plan to spare me the scorn of my peers had one central flaw—headgear. Despite the orthodontist's instructions stipulating that I should only wear the full-skull scaffolding at night, Ma affixed them to my face during the school day as well, in order to ensure we got our money's worth.

I was entering third grade now, and our mornings started with squabbles over what to wear. I'd emerge from our jumbled closet in Baba's old OPEC sweater, and Ma would reprimand me, "You want everyone to think we're poor? That I can't dress you in new clothes?"

Ma ripped the sweater off over my head, snagging the headgear on the way off, then stuffed me into a Blue Angels F-18 sweatshirt and gray sweatpants ensemble. She failed to notice the jets on the shirt, which meant it was for a boy, but no matter, it had been on sale and was enough sizes too big that I could grow into it. If that wasn't bad enough, she hiked the bottom half of the outfit to my bellybutton and tucked the sweatshirt in to give me what she referred to as a "tidy" appearance. To complete the indignity, she matched a pair of fresh white socks and penny loafers, then stepped back to observe her styling. She nodded approvingly, apparently pleased with herself.

I turned reluctantly to the vanity mirror and burst into tears. When someone says they were a homely child, they never saw me. I had beady eyes behind bottle-cap glasses, a monorail of headgear, and a nerdy boy's sweatpants outfit on.

"At least take the headgear off!" I groveled.

Unmoved, Ma sent me down to the bus stop at the end of the road anyway. I waddled the whole way, trying to calm my overexcited waistline. If I'd been the bus driver that day, I would not have stopped for the misshapen, angry little person waiting under the "No Trespassing" sign.

Dread filled me on the approach to school. I wore my hood up through the hallway and entered my new classroom, ready for a hail of laughing sounds. But the principal came on the intercom and asked us all to stand for the Pledge of Allegiance before anyone noticed me. I shuffled up from my seat and moved my mouth, pretending I knew the words to what everyone was saying. Crystal, my desk buddy, pinched me and showed me how to hold my hand over my heart. After the pledge, Mrs. Newton pulled down a world map in front of the chalkboard and affixed its hook to a nail. She then pointed out the fat boot next to Africa. "This is the Persian Gulf," she said, circling the Gulf with her finger, "and *this* is Kuwait." She pointed at a shape on the map, meaningless to her and everyone else in the room but me. I squirmed in my desk, trying to stop my hand from shooting up to correct her. Mrs. Newton glanced at me and then smiled around the room, not wanting to draw more attention than necessary to the scaffolding on my face.

"Now I know you all heard about the war on the news, and maybe your parents talked to you about it . . . has anyone seen the big army airplanes in the sky lately?"

Most of the class murmured yes to this question. By now I was now kneeling on top of my desk, waving my hand in the air.

"Yes Sophia. What is it?"

"It's not the Persian Gulf. It's the Arabian Gulf!" I corrected breathlessly.

"Can you explain to me why on this map it is the Persian Gulf and on the news they call it the *Persian* Gulf? Pretty official."

"I don't know! It just is." I was glowing from the warmth of my conviction. Impertinent and cranky, I jumped up and ran to the map, took a moment to find Qatar, and pointed at the little thumb jutting out into the *Arabian* Gulf. "This is where I used to live. My baba, I mean my *dad*, is from here," I exclaimed, taking care to use the American term for father.

Mrs. Newton was about to respond but was interrupted by Bri Barker in the back, "Hey, railroad mouth! Is Saddam your *dad*?"

I leveled a death stare from over the construction on my face.

"Is that how come Sophia don't know the Pledge of Allegiance? Cause Saddam's her dad?" Crystal asked, half-ratting, half-curious.

"Enough!" was all Mrs. Newton had to offer in my defense, and she changed the subject. "Everyone, take your earth science books out. This week we're going to start reading about Pangaea!"

11

EPSILON BOÖTIS •
THE LOINCLOTH • الإزار

With Ma's various temp jobs stacking up, she was home less and less of the time. By now I was beginning fifth grade and I know breasts were a major concern of the time, because I began keeping a journal and wrote about them *a lot*. I kept monologues on cup sizes and other profound thoughts in a notebook with a holographic cover. My entries were vague, but the project of mapping out my own private hinterland was explicit. I poured into it my secret pubescent thoughts and opinions about *all* of the strange new world that was opening up to me. Cable TV, adult magazines in the corner store, and the conversations of my ten- and eleven-year-old classmates filled the notebook. Class chat was all rumors trickled down from older siblings and misheard lyrics from songs on the radio. Although I was never included in these discussions, I recorded my observations as meticulously as a Victorian explorer drawing diagrams and explanatory foot-notes. I desperately wanted to have a window into the exotic world of sex and learn its language, customs, and costumes for myself.

I wrote these concerns down into the book in incriminating

block letters of plain English, even though I *knew* somewhere in the back of my mind that these were *1984*-style thoughtcrimes. The notebook was full of damning evidence manifest in the form of questions I shouldn't have been asking. I wrote about what I imagined lurking inside the little store's Saran-wrapped copies of *Hustler* or beneath the glowing scramble of Spice TV. The diary became increasingly incriminating as I drew bizarre illustrations of body parts and disguised them in code—ice creams topped with cherries were my visual slang for "boobs," lightning bolts burst from jeans to represent "penis." One ballerina had labia that hung down so low from under her tutu I bound them up in pink slippers to make them look like an extra pair of legs. I approached my explorations in a spirit of scientific inquiry. Somehow I hoped this would pardon me should anyone find the journal. Then one day, a partial answer to my questions about adult anatomy came. Nestled in with a bunch of windowed bill envelopes, bank ads for personalized dolphin-art checkbooks, and Columbia House ads was a Frederick's of Hollywood catalogue, my Rosetta stone to a cartoonishly commodified world of sex! I dropped the boring mail onto the buffet and went straight to the bedroom, where I spent the rest of the afternoon Sharpie-ing *hijabs* onto the heads of the *almost* all-nude girls. Fantasy trumped all in this colorful compendium of glossy, posed female sexuality. The models reminded me of My Little Ponies, each with a special outfit of lacey dressage, manes over withers, round rumps, and plasticky, powder-soft skin. But while the boxes of My Little Ponies came clearly labeled "KEEP AWAY FROM SMALL

CHILDREN," the Frederick's catalogue had no warning of any choking hazard. I decided it was mine to keep.

Obsessed by my new discovery, I catalogued and mapped the hieroglyphics, learning to identify different kinds of lingerie (teddy, romper, waspie) and copying down their attendant constellation of adjectives (strappy, dentelle, crotchless). Within a few weeks I'd absorbed all the charge out of my secret catalogue. I began slicing the models up into little pieces and repurposed the mutilated bodies into collages of half-nude mermaids and centauresses, à la *Fantasia*. Using the bits of body to create fleshy chimeras in the diary, the girl in pasties became a half-zebra, and the blonde in red lace ended up an orange mermaid. But once I started collaging with the risqué photos, the evidence scattered in the garbage and on the floor was a giveaway to Ma. And the fact is, diaries inevitably get read. Usually by the last person in the world you would want to read them. Coming home from school one day, I knew something was wrong. It felt as though the pressure had dropped in the house, and I found her, red-faced, in the closet where I'd hidden my diary. It was a lesson learned, she said, for both of us. Then, in true thought-police form, she ordered me to rip every page with anything *haram*, or forbidden, on it out of the diary. By this time, Islam had become a convenient tool for Ma to keep us in line.

In most parenting matters Ma was self-sufficient. Now she spoke to other parents and even consulted Baba about the right line of action to take with me. "I don't understand where it is coming from!" she fretted over the phone to him.

"It is disturbing to me, Matar! Maybe it's all this stuff she sees on the TV, just the environment she's in here. Kids these days are just different." Baba prescribed a variety of remedies, including an increased intake of Quran and the possibility of another relocation to Doha, where I could live with Umi Safya. I was barely eleven, Ma pointed out, and she could never let me go on my own. My twinkling of sexual curiosity had obviously spooked her deeply. By the end of fifth grade our relationship had disintegrated into a permanent standoff. "It's only a phase," Gramma reassured Ma. But my "phase" wouldn't go away.

Ma's vigilance only drove me further underground and sharpened my moody conviction that I was being unfairly persecuted. Even after the school year had passed, I wanted nothing more than to get away from the scene of my thoughtcrime and wished Baba would scrape the funds together to buy me a ticket to Doha. I began writing everything in the diary out phonetically in Arabic script, my own private language even Dima couldn't read, my own evasive Navajo code.

During this time I passed into middle school and entered the sixth grade. This was the official end of childhood, American public school's exile from the nursery. Whatever molten hormones run in the veins of preteens were running hot in mine when school started that year. At that age there is a nonvolition, an unknowing of oneself that causes actions to come out inexplicable and divine. I moved, spoke, and acted without meaning and without meaning to; my fights with Ma, Dima, and even Gramma became frequent and caused everyone to walk rhythmlessly around me for fear of an attack. While cage-fighting with Dima usually ended in bloody wounds, and spitting at Ma only got me a slap across the face, I didn't mean any of it.

I started to fill my time after school loitering at the public library. I noticed that most people came to the librarians with missions. They needed a particular episode of *Red Dwarf* or wanted to search this new thing called the Internet. I didn't know what I was looking for until I found it.

I must have paused ten times or more on *The Rise and Fall of Ziggy Stardust and the Spiders from Mars* before I decided to check it out. I took it home and promptly forgot about it in the bottom of my backpack full of library swag. It wasn't until one lonesome lunch period while pretending to be busy cleaning my bag out that I found it again. I locked myself in the bathroom (the most private place on campus), and pressed play. By the second song, it was "Soul Love," and by the time I'd committed "Rock 'n' Roll Suicide" to memory, I was long gone (and so turned on). My devotion to Bowie was immediate and earnest and fervent, in the way only twelve-year-old virgins can truly *love* a pop idol. Of course I was decades too late to freak out in his moon-age daydream, be one of his young Americans, or put on a pair of red shoes and dance the blues, but I still *believed* this album was made for me. The spangled guitars, the piano romps, and the emotional sway of that voice going from a low crackle to a shrill howl gave me the kind of all-powerful shivers in the groin (even off that crappy cassette tape) that made other girls at my school scream and faint over Garth Brooks or Boys II Men. Vising the metal band of my headphones onto my ears and disguising them around the house under a beanie, I wrapped myself into a clinging embrace with the album and didn't let go until it was overdue.

The way Bowie emancipated a word like "sparkle" from being a boring marketing term aimed at girls in my age bracket, turning it into a sexy secret, inspired me to start writing in my journal again. The possibility of subverting my mother's all-seeing eye and making up new and obscure innuendos was my new goal in the writing. At the back of the book I carefully took dictation from the tape, copying down the cut-up sublogic of the lyrics into my expurgated diary. I alternated my set of Japanese glitter gel pens for a rainbow effect and drew a pink star for words I either couldn't decipher or didn't want Ma to read.

I suppose it was the idea of a concept album that was most mind-boggling to me, as were the possibilities of creating an alter ego or curating one's own personal mythology. For all homely, zit-faced, graceless people, the notion that a different, unrecognizable, *other* version of yourself might be possible is both the most liberating and the most seductive of beliefs. David Bowie went from the gross codpiece-wearing goblin prince in *Labyrinth* to my spiritual icon in the course of a few weeks. I couldn't let the album just go back into public circulation! I had to keep it with me—*always*. I took one of Baba's Quran cassettes and taped the songs of darkness and dismay right over the top of Surat Al-Baqara, and the more I listened, the more fervent my devotion became.

I set about building my own alter ego from the sale racks of Value Village and the suitcases of old clothes from Doha. Where I had previously paid acute attention to the cliques I might fit into—preps, hillbillies, skaters, D&D gamers, and so on—by spring I had built a remarkably unflattering wardrobe of secondhand crap and had split all of Dima's old *jalabiyas* at the seams by trying to wear them as shirts. The closet was a mixture of ninety-nine-cent tropical sunset shirts, wrinkled old *hijabs*, pin-on epaulettes, broken sunglasses, and polyester leisure suits. My most precious acquisition had been a pair of American flag Converse—striped on the sides in red and white, blue tongue speckled with white stars—which I wore with a pair of slouch-crotch *sirwal* with thick silver cuffs embroidered up to my knees. The first time I wore them outdoors we had already walked halfway to school before Dima observed, "Those pants make you look like you pooped yourself."

Still disturbed by my diary, Ma now found a new source of disgust in my clothing. The glitter-grunge-via-Gulf look gave her cause to tell me on repeat that she hadn't worked long and hard to clothe me in perfectly good *new* clothing from K-Mart just to have me turn around and wear dirty hand-me-downs on purpose. She took it as a slap in the face to her efforts and took special offense to hair experimentation involving peroxide, egg white, and the ultimate contraband: Manic Panic.

"You look ridiculous," Ma growled, snapping the elastic bands off my head. "You need to keep a lower profile," she warned. "There are predators *on the lookout* for girls like you!" Ma believed that all the pedophiles in the county were waiting for us just beyond the property line and that they were somehow organized and monitoring the routes to and from our school with walkie-talkies. "Are you *trying* to draw attention to yourself?" Of course I was, though I wouldn't admit it. She tugged at my glow-in-the-dark alien guitar-pick necklace and broke the mint dental floss I'd used to tie it around my neck. "You *want* to look like a freak?" *Duh*, I thought to myself, and answered, "I'd rather look like a freak than look like you."

She froze with a look as though I'd just stabbed her in the heart. I shrank back as Ma cast around for something of value to me. Her eyes locked on my box of tapes. I lunged to protect them, but she was too quick. She fingered through my carefully curated collection of mixtapes from the radio and pirated copies from the library. She picked out *Ziggy* and held it up as an example to me, then hooked her finger under the magnetic strip. I screamed, falling instantly into hysterics as she pulled out a long strand of tape as she unwound the album, brown tape glimmering as she spooled it round her fist and ripped it out at the reel.

"You want attention from dangerous men? Okay! You want to end up cut into pieces and dead in a ditch? Be my guest!" Ma had grown up in an era (and an area) where dressing like a hippie tramp was less liberating than it was dangerous.

She moved on now to my other cassettes: Nirvana's *Unplugged in New York*, *One in a Million* by Aaliyah, a copy of Orson Welles's *War of the Worlds* broadcast from the local PBS station. All the while she was clenching her teeth and swearing under her breath. Something about "no daughter of mine is going to turn out a freak." She finished off, leaving only the tapes she had bought me for my birthday, *Wolf Songs* and Wagner's *Die Walküre*—perfect for the howling fugue I had worked myself up into.

THE GIRL WHO FELL TO EARTH

Then, with a calmness that seemed maniacal to me, she concluded, "You're not going to be able to get a job dressed like that."

"I'm not *trying* to get a job!" I choked through my snot while I wept over the mangled tapes on the floor.

"You're going to need one if you're going to stay under *this* roof!"

"But I'm twelve!"

"You want to keep buying this garbage? Fine. But I'm not paying for any of it!" We eyed each other tensely, each waiting for the other to move. Tears were now trickling down over my crumpled chin. "I'd been earning my keep for years by the time I was your age! Now go clean yourself up."

In that unfortunate moment, I got up from my nest of dead cassettes and I wiped my snot and tears and the makeup I was expressly forbidden from wearing across my cheeks.

"Is that *mascara?*" Ma roared.

Sniveling, I made a rookie error and lied, "No!"

That was it. Busted.

"*Just* for lying to me, you are going to go into this closet right now and throw out every piece of junk you've collected." Ma dragged out a mound of my Salvation Army artifacts and began plowing through it.

Her anger and my hysteria escalated as she discovered the extent of my horde. An electric-blue bowling bag, a silky Chinese restaurant delivery jacket with a dragon embroidered on the back, moldy *Camelot 3000* comic books from the '80s, some cheap plastic costume jewelry from Saudi, and all the rest of my fledgling hipster paraphernalia were stuffed into a Hefty bag. Ma carried it out to the trash and forced it in, spraying the hose into the garbage can so I wouldn't go through it trying to rescue anything.

That night, after Ma had gone to work, I stayed awake well past midnight watching MTV to spite her. I didn't hear her engine approach outside, didn't hear the brake crunch or the car door slam, or any of the Pavlovian triggers that usually warned me to turn the radio down and change the channel. For these occasions I kept a *Cosmos* tape in the VCR, so if I were watching anything verboten I could switch back to our approved TV chaperone, Carl Sagan, and Ma would never know. But getting caught was an inevitability under Ma's surveillance, and just as Æon Flux somersaulted across the screen in her bondage harness, legs spread-eagled, tits like two stiff torpedoes, I felt the rocking chair pull back. I knew it was over before I had time to switch to Carl's model of a tesseract. That night Ma was on the phone to Baba arranging a ticket for me to leave.

12

BETA COLUMBAE COLUMBA •
THE WEIGHT • الوزن

The flight from SeaTac Airport to Amsterdam Schiphol took half a day, and then it was another seven hours to Abu Dhabi and forty-five minutes to Doha. Hemmed into Schiphol's international nowhere land of travel-size cosmetics and mutant Toblerone chocolate, I felt free. Riding miles up and down the terminal concourse on a walkalator gave me my first taste of autonomy. But my blissful float was tainted by the knowledge that I was en route to a place where privacy amounted to five minutes alone in the bathroom once a day. Yes, the airport of Amsterdam was the one place I was going to have the chance to transgress consequence-free.

I went into the news kiosk with my twenty emergency guilders and hovered timidly near the brink where Art/Lifestyle dropped brow into Men's Interest/Porn. I emerged with an oversized European fashion magazine full of nightlife photography and interviews in a language I couldn't read but whose subjects were fabulous beyond words. The portraits were variously taken in lofts and luxury hotels; floor-length windows revealed views of city skylines I pretended I might be en route to. I parked myself at a gate bound for

Paris and leafed through the thickly glossed pages. It was most precious for its dazzling color and surreal imagery, suspending me for hours while I waited in the terminal. There were models posed to play random female icons: Elizabeth I in a brocade pantsuit, the Virgin Mary in a red maillot and blue beach towel, Joan of Arc chrome-clad in Mugler body armor.

I knew this magazine full of scantily clad women would be contraband and, therefore, our time was limited together. Self-censorship had become habitual after the journal incident in fifth grade, so I decided not to try to bring it into the Gulf and set about rigorously memorizing the delicious details of each photograph. Time folded around me, and before I'd made it halfway through the magazine, boarding was announced. Final call came over the intercom while I hunched deeply over the last spread, titled "Grow Up" in English. It was shot on a playground; women in couture slid down slides, rode seesaws, and climbed trees. The last image was of a model captured midair as she launched from a swing. I left her on my seat reluctantly, where she stayed permanently suspended and artfully akimbo in a slit red dress.

I was still brooding over having to leave my magazine in Amsterdam when I emerged onto the catwalk of Abu Dhabi International Airport, suitcase jittering across the studded rubber tile behind me. Customs hadn't even bothered scanning my luggage, and I had passed through the stand of security guards as if I were invisible. The men who guarded the sliding doors marked "UAE Border" had way bigger problems than a kid with a magazine full of artistic nude pictures.

I joined the parade of other passengers milling toward the parking lot. As we passed into the arrivals hall I felt the sharpness of a thousand eyes pecking me out like a painted bird. They craned over the railing, Indian and Arab men silently expressing everything from mild curiosity to personal offense at my bare, bony legs. It had been a really long time since I'd seen my father's face, and now I reminded myself of his identifying features. He was a brown man with a mustache . . . but so was everyone else here. Each configuration of facial hair and skin tone along my path was different, but none of them was the one I was looking for. I tried to hold an image of him in my head and clenched my mind around it like a fist. But it was like holding a handful of sand. All the half-recollected details of his face just slipped away.

Then it occurred to me with panicked alarm, "What if *he* doesn't recognize *me*?" The changes in my body had been pretty abstract until now. I felt my new height and my new heft and the hairiness of my legs. For the first time I took stock of my short haircut, my greasy face that needed washing, and these American clothes that suddenly made me feel indecently exposed. Like an animal sinking into a tar pit, my body felt like a burden. I slowed as I came to the end of the hall, each step heavier as I neared the exit. Were the soles of my shoes melting to the floor, or was I just tired?

The sweat of bodies folded over me in a heady arbor—the distinct aroma of the Arabian Gulf. Even now the scent of salty perspiration laced with *oud* has a soporific effect on me. It is the smell of my father's armpits and, thus, an elusive port of safety. If I didn't recognize his face, maybe I'd recognize his smell. I found an empty spot on a marble ledge and fell asleep in the shade of a plastic palm tree like some postmodern pastoral scene—dozing shepherdess replaced by jetlagged young traveler.

When I woke the airport was quieter and Baba was rousting me out of the pebble-filled planter and leading me to the car. "You were early," he said as he buckled me into the passenger seat. I pretended to be asleep and peered at him through my eyelashes. He looked like the photo we had over the hearth in Gramma's house. Stern and silent.

Hesitant to let on I was awake, I grasped for the appropriate way to address him or a greeting to open the floodgates of the father-daughter conversation I imagined we were supposed to have, the kind that TV dads had with TV kids in their TV homes. But when nothing came to mind I resolved it was best to remain in stasis. Tomorrow I could start over, I thought. I could wake up and say good morning as though only a night had passed since we'd left him. I practiced this in my head, planning to kiss his cheek and give him a hug. But these thoughts were crushed in a bottleneck of nameless emotion fizzing up in my throat. I yawned to pop the pressure in my ear and rolled over to face the window. Tall streetlamps studded the desert road in a nauseating rhythm and tears puddled on my cheeks. Before they fell I felt his hand vise the nape of my neck, just like he used to do when pulling my teeth—it worked like some kind of Vulcan nerve pinch. The reeling stopped and I began to drift, this time peacefully, orange light dashing me into the darkness, mind steadying to a place where nothing was the matter and everything was forgiven.

Next morning I awoke at sunrise in a familiar bed, the

old one from our flat in the city with a scalloped headboard painted with fluffy clouds. The room was empty but for a mirror and a baby's crib. The walls were covered in stickers and crayon markings, signs of my *other* siblings. I wondered where they were and then I wondered how many there were. Ma and Baba had a mutually enforced "Don't Ask, Don't Tell" policy about Flu's pregnancies, but I guessed from the crib that there had been a few new additions. Beside the bed was a new *jalabiya*, a polyester slip, a *fanila*, some barrettes, a copy of *Majid* comics, and a black *shala* to cover my hair with.

I picked up the cotton *fanila*, tiny rosettes stitched along the neck. Leaving me an undershirt was proof Baba hadn't expected me to have grown into a B-cup. The slip fit fine, but static made it stick to the hair on my legs like Velcro. A pretty girl modeled a tastefully striped nightie on the cover of the *jalabiya* packaging. But the garment I pulled from the plastic bore no resemblance to the one she was wearing. I popped my head out the itchy neckhole and looked in the mirror to find a shapeless mass of fabric patterned with strange cartoon creatures of indeterminate phylum. No matter how I tried to flatten it, the stiff white ruff stuck up around my face and made me feel like a dog in a funnel collar. Last I picked up the *shala*, my first veil, nested in with an array of kids' clothing. Despite the fabric being incredibly light, the veil held a heavy musk of ambergris. I wrapped it around my head several times into a loose wimple as I'd seen the women in the airport do, but when I let go it just slipped away into a limp coil around my neck.

Baba was sitting on the floor with a newspaper and

breakfast of pocket bread and eggs. "*Marhaba! Benti!*" he cried, and held out his hands for me like he was receiving a present. Bending down for a kiss on the cheek, I gave him an electrical shock instead. "Wow, you get so big!" I could hear the echoes of Gramma in his bad English. I folded myself down beside him. "Ha? Tell me. What you will do this summer?" He dealt me a piece of bread over the swirl of egg.

"I dunno," I grunted. "Aren't I going to stay here with you?"

"*Wella*, you know, I thought you can stay here with me. But you are so grown up now." I caved my chest back and hoped he wouldn't notice I needed a bra. "I think you might be happier if you go to Doha and stay with Umi Safya."

I looked around the flat; it was almost completely empty. The only decoration was a glow-in-the-dark Mecca clock hanging on the wall over his head, the minute and hour hands ticking from the center of the *Kaaba*. "Did you just move here or something?"

He got up to make me a cup of tea. "No. I been here, maybe three years."

"Then how come there's no furniture? How come no one is here?"

"This is the living," he answered. "If I want to go, I just go. You know your baba." He smiled at me.

"You find the *shala*?" I nodded. "Good. It's a gift from Abir. You remember Abir?"

I tensed. Baba loved to test me on my knowledge of the extended tribal tree. I filed through my hazy memory of relatives, Abrar, Alia, Afra, Afia, sure, but I came up blank at the name Abir.

"Abir! You must remember! You met her when you were little in Saudi."

I slowly ripped my bread, hoping he'd change the subject. He clicked his tongue as though he were ashamed. I was starting to worry this was some kind of a riddle—maybe I *should* know her. "What's her face like?" I tried.

He looked at me as if I were an idiot. "How should I know? I've never seen her face." Sufficiently convinced it wasn't a trick question, I went back to my egg while Baba explained. "She is my father's—that's your grandfather Jabir—milk-brother's son's wife's sister by marriage."

I gulped, trying to digest both the eggs and the flimsy familial tissue linking myself to the nice (faceless) lady who had given me the gift of the *shala*. "What's a milk-brother?"

"If your mother couldn't give you milk when you are a baby and you drank from a different mother, you would be milk-sister to her other children," he explained patiently.

Suddenly, the stillness of the room was broken with a loud racket from the hallway. It was a pack of children surging up the stairs, knocking every door they passed on the way up. I got up to investigate and peeked into the dim stairwell where a rabble of boys and girls, all in mini-*thobes* and *jalabiyas* in varying states of dirtiness, were playing keep-away with a balloon. It floated up and down the landing, and the kids, the oldest of whom couldn't have been more than seven, tumbled after it. They didn't see me, all eyes on the gently floating orb, little fists brandishing pencils, keening for the first jab.

"Who are they?" I asked, quietly closing the door so as not to draw their attention.

"Your cousins."

I remembered that *cousin* was a term used loosely here. "Why are they awake?" It was 6 a.m. at the latest. Baba shrugged. The stampede shook the ceiling like an earthquake. "Do they go to school?"

"Mostly the families here don't have *jinsia*, so they can't go to school."

I understood the word *jinsia*. It meant the very essence of a person's being, your sex, your personality, your nationality, your identity, and, in this situation, citizenship. "Is that why Flu and the kids stay in Doha?"

"Yes."

A loud detonation of helium came from the stairwell, followed by the siren-like howl of one of the littlest kids. Baba ignored the sound, plopping in several spoonfuls of sugar to sweeten the tea. He poured it from glass to glass for me as though I were still a little kid liable to scald herself.

"Is there anyone my age here?"

"No girls are here now. All of them are in Doha or Saudia for the summer break."

He handed me the tepid, syrupy tea and rattled off names of cousins I could visit with there. "Also your Auntie Falak. Flu. Your little sisters."

I got up to skulk by the window. Even though the prospect of spending three months in these empty rooms surrounded by the noise of the feral cousins depressed me, I wanted to stay a while longer.

I surveyed the turf. We were surrounded by undeveloped desert, sliced to the south by the highway to Abu Dhabi and to the north by power lines. The apartment we were in was part of a larger complex of buildings, each one an identical, squat square. They were similar in design to a council-estate scheme—well-intentioned but badly planned, all full of utopian details that only worked in the model. For example, the shopping arcades running underneath each building probably looked great in balsa wood. But where the mock-up would have been bustling with miniature commerce, the real places turned into creepy corridors full of garbage, with sand collecting along the unused shop fronts. This place, I would learn, was mostly full of Bedouin like Baba who for various reasons (political or financial or just by accident) found themselves on the periphery of society. Even in Doha they lived in zones of temporary-turned-permanent government housing and spent their lives waiting for jobs or the call to prayer or their favorite TV show to come on.

There was a derelict playground directly under our window. At the center was a flatbed merry-go-round creaking slowly in the wind. I imagined its steel heating up in the sun, just waiting for some hapless kid to come along and sear their flesh on the handlebars. Instead of wanting to run down and have a go on the swings, I just felt a churning twist of self-conscious dread that I was getting too old for it. Across the courtyard, a little girl pressed her face to a window. She smeared her forehead along the glass, pouting down at the playground that taunted her.

"Well, you're a grown-up now, Safya, what you decide? Go stay with the women in Doha or stay here alone?" Baba interrupted my observation.

A pair of hands removed the little girl from her perch at

the window. I wondered how many girls were even given a choice?

"I'll go."

The next day he took me back to the airport and checked me in, then found a pay booth near the entrance, where he called ahead to Doha. I leaned against the window watching businessmen get into taxis and migrant laborers load onto buses. A big beast of a Rolls Royce steamed up. Its windows were tinted dusky purple; it rode low on its chassis and the wide body was painted pearlescent white. Mesmerized, I wandered away down the hall to get a view of the front of the car while Baba negotiated a place for me in Umi Safya's crowded house. The grill gleamed, grinning like a huge albino crocodile. Paralyzed with curiosity, I watched as a female driver in a chauffeur's uniform stepped out against the wind and opened the back door to release a violent burst of flapping black fabric. And like birds escaping the croc's belly, a family of Emirati women emerged from the red-leather interior, leaving a scurry of porters to unload their luggage. I watched, readjusting my own unruly *shala* as theirs whipped frantically around their heads and yet stayed improbably in place. The skein swept in V-formation through the departure hall. Their floor-skimming *abayas* disguised their gait so that for a moment before they disappeared into the first-class area I believed they might be flying.

Dazzled by the display I'd just witnessed, I returned to Baba's side just as he hung up the phone. "Who were *they*?" I asked him, gawking after the fancy ladies.

"Don't look to them," he cautioned, and maneuvered me

in the opposite direction, toward the economy-class terminal entrance.

"When you get to Doha your uncle Faraj will pick you up. Do you remember him?"

"Ugh. I *think* so," I lied, wanting to avoid another confusing genealogical breakdown.

"You remember your auntie Falak?"

This one I knew. "Yes!"

He was unimpressed. "Falak and Faraj are twins."

"OK. Got it," I confirmed, like I was memorizing a mission.

"Your Uncle Faraj is getting married in Saudi Arabia at the end of the summer. That is the next time I will see you. *N'zayn?*"

The warble of a sob seized my throat. "*N'zayn.*"

I lingered in a window as Baba returned to his illegally parked rental sedan. The wind was getting stronger. He had to hold his *gutra* down to keep it from blowing away in the wind. He turned once to wave good-bye and then stepped in and drove off. I stayed brooding at the window, writing my name backward, then erasing it in the condensation, until my gate for Doha was called.

13

ETA URSAE MAJORIS •
DAUGHTERS OF THE BIER • بنات النعش

It's difficult to explain what it's like to be welcomed home
to a place you've never been. The levels of excitement when
I reached the house were totally disproportionate to how
I felt. Sounds and smells resonated strongest, a familiarity
that felt like it came from a dream. Cousins my age like Alia
were already wearing *abayas* and seemed preternaturally old
to me. The names and faces were the same but now they
were shy, unsure of how to treat me. Alia held a baby on her
hip and looked at least eighteen. It was as though a childhood spent caring for younger siblings while her parents
floundered in adjustment to city life had made this twelve-
year-old girl a matron.

The living room was full of people, and as I passed into
their arms they adorned me with bangles and anointed me
with perfume and stuffed handfuls of candy into my pockets. I was taken to my grandmother, who sat on the floor at
the center of the room flanked by her eldest daughters, my
aunts Moody and Zayna. She lifted the corner of her black
berga and exposed her smooth cheek, offering it up to me for

a kiss. I remembered this same gesture from when I met her in the tent in the desert in Saudi.

"Welcome to your home," she said, and held my arm tight while she manacled a heavy silver bangle onto my wrist.

Despite the grand welcome, I could barely gather the corners of my mouth up into a smile of gratitude. It was an inexplicably angsty moment shadowed with a vague suspicion of walking into some kind of a trap.

Cousins whom I remembered by face but not name hugged close, battling to sit near me. They touched my short hair and ransacked my suitcase and talked at me even though I didn't understand. If we'd had a language barrier before, I couldn't remember it. When we were young I guessed we must have just spoken to one another in our respective languages, happy not to understand before falling into a game of double dutch. Now that we were too old for jump rope, we compared the tone of our skin, measured ourselves back-to-back, and grinned stupidly at one another. These, after all, were the things that transcended language.

I was led into the back of the house, where I was shown into all the bedrooms one by one and where women I didn't recognize (new wives of old uncles) were nursing, changing diapers, or sleeping. As we wound through the hallway it seemed to go on and on like a warren. A wide door papered with a giant poster of a desert island stuck out conspicuously at the end of the hallway.

"Whose room is that?" I asked, pointing to the metal handle that ripped through the beach.

"Right now only Faraj. Next month, his bride."

"That makes four new brides in the house," someone tallied up.

If I hadn't already observed it, this drove home that the living conditions were tight. I was allotted half a bunk in Aunt Falak's room and was relieved to see her perched atop a steel bunk bed watching TV.

"*Marhaba*, Sweyfiya!" she said, twisting "Safya" up into an affectionate pet name and spreading her arms in welcome. I climbed up the ladder to give her a kiss. "*Burra!*" she screeched at the kids who had followed me in, and shut the door behind them. "You can come in here if you want to be alone, okay?"

I agreed to her offer and slept off my jet lag while she resumed watching *Predator 2* and occasionally banging the door to scare off the kids whispering mysteriously to each other in the hall.

It's a common misconception that all Gulf Arabs are rich. So I feel the need here to lay out the fact that our family absolutely was and is not. Marginalized from the moment borders, cities, and politics began to solidify in the Gulf, Bedouin families like those in Al-Dafira had a difficult time adapting to urban life. In the '80s, the governments of many Gulf countries had planned boroughs and filled them with relocated Bedouin. Parts of the Al-Dafira tribe had been crossing back and forth through the neck of the peninsula between Saudi and Qatar, Kuwait and the UAE for generations. While the disorienting effects of industry and modernity dizzied the tribe, invisible lines were being drawn in the sand under their feet and on the papers they couldn't read. Sides of the border were taken and families were broken up. Each patriarch had to choose his nationality: Saudi or Qatari or Emirati? For those who chose Qatar, they each received one house called a *beit shaabi*. These "folk houses" were stocky one-story blocks set back behind twelve-foot-tall walls of concrete erected to protect the women's privacy. What they didn't factor in was that out in the desert, there was no privacy. Even if men and women socialized separately, things were much more fluid than "culturally sensitive" urban planning allowed for. There were two living rooms for each house: a *majlis* for the men and a *sala* for the women. And like a labyrinth opening out, once you passed through the public area of the women's section, there was a long turned hallway with five doors that led on to bedrooms, packed with blankets and carpets and coffee pots and all the trappings of old life—everything shoved into a room with a large bed that was in turn piled at night with at least one family of four to each.

The house seemed to be permanently under construction; whenever another down-and-out family member needed a place to sleep, they just knocked the walls out to add a back room. In the desert this would have been easy— weave another flap, add another meter to the tent—but on a government-supplied block of land they had to be secretive about it. Thus the lean-to and the low-ceilinged cinder-block rooms jutted out of the main house and hunched below the line of the outer wall so no one would know they had been built. Despite the crowded house I did end up steeping myself in a copy of *Dune* that I had stowed away in my suit-case, if for nothing else than to comfort myself with a bit of English amid the all-guttural Bedu Arabic I was slowly start-ing to pick up. Between chapters I watched *Carrie* and *Hell-raiser* and other rated-R horror films with Falak and played Super Nintendo in the *majlis*, neither of which required any subtitling. This was at the beginning of the Arabsat satellite TV revolution in the Middle East, and we watched things I'd *never* have been allowed to see under Ma's watch. Against all usual notions of cultural permissiveness, Doha was surpris-ingly free for me compared to Puyallup. There was no cur-few, no diet, and no one able to read my diary. I was as happy as I ever remembered being as the days of the first month slipped by in a hallucinatory dream of boisterous evenings in the *sala* and quiet mornings reading from Herbert. I began to fantasize about living there; it was chaos, but it was nice to have nothing whatsoever expected of me. Still, the no-tion that I might fit into the tribe for longer than a summer vacation was false. For the moment, my place was honorary and free, like Paul Atreides being tolerated at first by the Fremen. But I'd have to prove myself with a longer stint of living there to become anything more than "the visitor."

Since I wasn't leaving the house much, my first big task was getting the lay of the clan. Falak and Alia dragged a box of photos out of an old metal trunk in Umi's room. They pointed faces out as we went through the black-and-white stacks. Alia pointed out our grandfather Jabir, *thobe* humbly short, *bisht* threadbare, beard surprisingly similar to the one worn by my grandfather Kaarle in his Klondike photo. This picture of my grandfather, with a broad *khanjar* and rifle strapped across his torso with leather straps, reminded me of the crysknives of *Dune* and sent my imagination spinning.

Farther into the trunk we found a studio photograph taken in Kuwait circa 1968. We saw Umi Safya with Mohamed, my uncle, and Matar, my father. Her face was covered with a leathery *berga*, but her long braids were out and layered over her shoulders. Silver rings studded her knuckles and at her knee was Baba, as spindly thin and skittish as a goat kid. He would have been nine. By then, Ma would have been driving a Ford Galaxie that guzzled fuel from the oil field her future husband was born on. Between 1968 and the present, the Gulf had sped up while America slowed down. Time was more precious here; perhaps that accounted for Alia and the other girls seeming to have aged faster than me. I felt like an astronaut landing back on earth and finding everyone she ever loved to be older. The wrinkles of the Gulf were premature and showed in everything I looked at, the decrepit streets and even the houses crumbling, though some were less than a decade old. And it showed in the relative maturity of my cousins, who, though many of them had never been to the downtown area of Doha, had to serve as the go-betweens for their parents in the transition from the desert to the city, helping the older generation to fill out paperwork, fix electrical outlets, and learn to work a washing machine.

While the rest of the Gulf was modernizing, our family had remained a time capsule of tradition or, depending on how some people felt about Al-Dafira, a bastion of backwardness. It was by going through Umi Safya's trunk that

I began to understand how close I had come to not being born at all. It would have been so easy for Baba to have stayed safely in this world he knew. It must have seemed so impossible, the thought of leaving. The fact that he did leave his home, fell in love with my mother, had me . . . it was all just so improbable.

We kept shuffling through photo after photo, some only a few years old and of family still living the old way in the desert. Falak laughed at a photo of herself as a baby riding bare-bottomed on Umi's shoulder, hair wild as a bird's nest on top of her tiny squinting face. In one photograph dated just the year before, the black gash of a hair-house tent was pitched against the faint vertical stripes of our new towering city in the distance. The little figures in the photo looked to me like time travelers.

Falak squinted into the photo, trying to make out who they were. "That's your brother Badr with the dog." She pointed him out.

"How can you tell?" I asked. The boy was facing away from the camera, clothed in a brown winter *thobe*.

Falak shrugged as though it were obvious. "The shape of his head, the way he's standing."

I stared long at the little figure but gleaned no clues. It seemed the uncanny gift of recognition that was hardwired into everyone else's brains had skipped me. Even as a child I remembered being confused by the veiled women all around me and felt a strange jealousy when still-crawling babies were able to pick their mothers out of a lineup of identically perfumed and identically veiled women. I thought that if by chance one generation and half a world were removed from the equation, I might have been living one of the last of the ancient ways on earth. I tried to express my thoughts to Falak and Alia, but they were only interested in a heart-shaped Gulf Colours flip-book full of wedding portraits.

Reading and writing in Arabic came back to me easily from when I had learned as a child. However, the guts to speak it didn't. At night I snuck onto the roof and sat amid the antennae and wires that ran through the dust. Up there I'd stare into the darkness and practice saying words aloud while the televisions blared downstairs. The vastness of the sky was less terrifying than in the open desert, but I still stayed close to the satellite dish in case I had to hang on to something to avoid falling up. The glottal stops and gargles just came out as odd amphibious croaks. When I wasn't on the roof doing my impression of Kermit the Frog reading Quran, I was lurking in the corners of rooms, surveilling the occupants. It was like being the Predator trying to activate camouflage into floral wallpaper: ridiculous. The complexities of the language, movements, and silent communication were impossible to imitate, despite my timid attempts at chirping into misunderstood conversations. My aunts rewarded my efforts at assimilation by not paying any attention to me, which was a relief. In America, being housebound meant a whole lot of navel-gazing. Now, even though I never left the house, I never once had to turn to myself for entertainment.

It was difficult to keep a firm grasp on the passing of days. No one was in school or working, so one morning blended in with the next, and before I'd gotten my footing, it had been a month. Late at night I snuck into the *majlis* to play *Mortal*

Kombat on Moody's sons' Nintendo. I wasn't supposed to be there—it had been years since the other girls had even been into the *majlis*—but I was new, so the house was lenient with me breaking these taboos.

Early one morning, more than a month into my stay, Ma called to inform me it was my birthday. I'd completely forgotten. She opened the phone call with, "Are you homesick yet?" trying to gauge if I'd been exorcised of my perverse Americanized interests yet.

"No. Not really. I love it so much here," I lied spitefully and sat back, wrapping my toes in the phone cord while she talked. "Thirteen years ago today . . ." she began as she always began her unexpurgated telling of my birth, which seemed to change slightly every year to include new details. The way she told me about my epic push through the birth canal made it sound as though I had forged the Northwest Passage.

"You squalled when they finally got you out. It was thundering and lightning outside because a summer storm started up."

I was eager to have a few practice rounds on the Nintendo, which I noticed was sitting beside the TV, dormant.

"And after they wiped you clean of all the mess, your Gramma held you up and looked into your big black eyes. And you know what she said?"

I cringed deeply, knowing the embarrassing line she was about to deliver.

"She said to me, 'Gale,' she said, '*that* is a wise baby.'"

It was then I began to notice a new, strange pain in my stomach that had been insinuating itself for days. "Can I go now?" I asked urgently, suddenly wanting to curl up into the fetal position.

"I didn't realize you were so busy." Her voice was tinged with hurt. "This is long-distance so . . . I miss you." Cruelly, I didn't reply and waited for her to hang up the phone.

Back in the women's quarters, Falak wrapped a *shala* around my eyes and led me through the house. I clutched my belly to warm up the aching part and followed her blindly into the living room, where she removed the scarf and yelled, "Surprise!" in my ear. A boom box squatted on top of the TV with a stack of tapes. The fixings looked more forlorn than festive. A shiny banner spelling out "MERRY XMAS" dangled from the doorjamb, and balloons sniffled along the confetti-strewn carpet like octopi on the seafloor.

"Thank you!" I grasped Falak in a sweaty hug.

"What will you wear?" she asked.

I shrugged. "This?" I looked down at the kitten-print *jalabiya* I hadn't changed in three days.

"No. No. It is a costume party." She held up a sari to illustrate. "I'll be a Bollywood starlet."

"What'll I be?" I asked. "I don't have a costume."

"That's easy," Falak answered. "You can be a *boyah* for your birthday." She went on to explain to me that a *boyah* was a tomboy.

The word was so much a part of daily parlance that no one seemed to make the connection that it was just a feminine conjugation of the English word *boy*.

"Like Princess Sapphire?" I asked her, equating the word to the mysterious cross-dressing anime heroine from my childhood in Apartment 1303.

"Exactly."

Falak cobbled together a costume for me from one of Moody's sons' crisp white *thobes*, a pair of mirrored aviator sunglasses pilfered from Faraj's room, and eyeliner, which she used to draw a mustache. The *gutra* was harder to keep on my head than a *shala*, and the billowy wide-legged *sirwal* made me feel disturbingly exposed. While she dressed me, Falak explained the origins of the *boyah*, which she claimed had begun in the university. In retrospect I gather that the combination of captivity and segregation had caused a sexually charged ecosystem to arise, similar to that of a women's prison. From this was born the *boyah*. Although there were no showers to drop soap in, it was best to avoid going into the university bathroom stalls alone. My imagination went wild while Falak described roving girl gangs with short hair and mustaches who ruled the campus, intimidating teachers and students alike. As with many gang cultures, *boyah* stylings had trickled down to the high schools of the city. But it became more than drag or inflecting your walk with butch swagger. There is a prismatic range of *boyah* types, from hetero-dabblers to the most earnest bull dyke.

After *Maghreb* prayer our guests started arriving. I stood off in a corner and received greetings. We mocked the way men kissed, nose-to-nose in a slightly aggressive version of an Eskimo uga-muga. One-two-three, we pecked, the number depending on how long it had been since we'd seen each other. The arrivals expanded out from first cousins to "clan-cousins"—which had become my private term for anyone of indeterminate relation. They came by the truckful, Suburbans and Nissans dropping the girls off at the door.

On entering the room everyone dropped their *abayas* to dramatically reveal themselves as doctors, tennis players, princesses, farm girls in straw hats, and even a tuxedo-clad vampire.

I flicked a *mesbah* around my forefinger, the sting of prayer beads pinching my knuckles, winding me up into a macho mood. Aunt Moody brought a tray of juice boxes around. I pulled a Vimto from the stack and punctured a hole in the carton, purple juice bubbling up and over onto my *thobe*.

"Don't get the *thobe* dirty! Vimto is harder to get out than blood," Moody warned.

The berry juice burst—a bright tang in my mouth—and I promised I'd be extra careful. Ma never used to allow us to drink the stuff; the taste was so vivid and the dye so dark she said it was practically poison and that back in America it was probably illegal.

Little kids bunched around me trying to wipe away my mustache. Aunt Moody stood guard at the door to make sure none of the boys broke in, and when they crawled onto the windowsill to peep, she shoved her *asa* through the grill at them. Falak plugged a mic into the boom box and the entertainments commenced. She emceed with ceremony, introducing each girl by her costume.

"*Ooo!* It's Dracula with his bride, Princess Jasmine." My aunt Zayna, the vampire, batted her cape (a cut-up *abaya*) and pretended to maul Princess Jasmine. Applause and hoots were milked from the peanut gallery piled around me.

"Allah! Woooow! Andre Agassi!" My cousin Aya bounced forth swinging a badminton racket. Next a figure in a pair of pajamas and a crappy latex mask shuffled forward, eliciting genuine shrieks from the littlest kids. "And this is . . ." Falak didn't know what to call it. Only mumbles escaped the mask. She barely held back laughter as the monster went and sat down out of the way. The boys had started rattling the window outside; Moody thwacked them away with her stick.

After dinner, some of the girls performed synchronized dances to the Kuwaiti band Miami and Egyptian megastar Amr Diab, although the music could barely be heard over the general mayhem of having almost forty women and children crammed into the living room. They jigged and reeled and did the electric slide and whipped their long hair back and forth. I was feeling woozy and vaguely nauseous; the ache in my belly was spreading. I made a break for the bathroom but when I got to the door, Moody stopped me. A nasal, old Saudi song came on.

"We need a man to dance to this one!" Moody said, and shoved me into the center of the room. Some of the other girls got up and waited for my lead.

"*Yella!* Dance!" They pushed me.

I held my elbow like I'd seen men do on TV and moved the sword up and down like a tollgate. My stomach wrenched and then fell into a numb relief. Just as I was starting to feel the a-rhythm of the *khaleeji* drumbeat, I realized that something slick was spreading down my leg. The clapping fell out of time and the air filled with whispers. I slowed my rock-step as another gush burst down the leg of the white cotton of the *sirwal*. I looked down at my front, pinpricks of a blackish red saturating out to form a thick streak on the white *thobe*. Fear, shock, and humiliation rolled through me in fast succession. Getting my first period was *way* worse than spilling Vimto on the *thobe*. Falak rushed me out of the room to help clean up the blood. She taught me how to rig a huge, three-inch-thick mattress of cotton up to my hips with clip-on bands.

The following week was spent just trying to forget what happened and trying to get comfortable. I was secluded in Falak's bedroom, too mortified from the public arrival of my "cycle," as everyone kept calling it, to venture out into the greater house. I cradled a hot water bottle over my belly and was served a steady diet of soup and hot tea. "Don't bathe," I was warned, "it just makes it take longer to go away." To entertain me in my convalescence, Falak broke out her collection of pirated Betamax tapes. She was stocked with 1980s horror films and Bollywood melodramas. She brought me a little pink package of pills. It reminded me of an oyster ridged with tiny white pearls. "One every day and *wella*, no more period!" I popped one and waited for it to cure me, turning the package over to read "contraception" printed crisply on the back. As it turned out, the doctors there prescribed the pill regularly to girls who complained of difficult periods, never telling them what it was actually for.

"So there are some things you should know now." Falak pulled a bag from her closet, broaching the subject nervously as though to remind me she was only the messenger. "You shouldn't go outside without *abaya* anymore."

She pulled an *abaya* from the bag. It was made of Crepe Lexus, a bionic, unwrinkleable black synthetic fabric from Japan. I tried it on blankly, wondering why she was so nervous about my reaction. I'd wrapped my head up in a *shala* and covered my face in a *berga* before, but this was the first time I'd tried on the full-body covering of an *abaya*.

"Thank you," I told her, and hung it on the coat hanger with hers.

"One other thing. You can't go into the *majlis* side of the house anymore."

Wearing *abaya* was fine with me—it was just an outfit—but being exiled from playing video games because I got my period seemed like punishment.

After that, I spent a lot of time lying beside Aunt Moody in the *sala* watching the TV on mute. "It didn't used to be like this," she said to cheer me up. "When your father and me were little, we used to run wild in the desert! Watching TV outside, howling at the moon with the Salukis." She seemed to brighten while she spoke. "We had nothing but a flap of goat hair between us and the stars—now we have this!" She slapped the thick cement wall separating the room we were in from the *majlis*. "In the old days, if I wanted to go for a walk with the goats, I went for a walk! As I preferred! In any direction I felt!"

In a single generation they had gone from migrating the peninsula with the seasons to living in windowless housing blocks. I pulled my knees up and popped my head into the neck of my *jalabiya* like a turtle. I was bloated and getting fat now. I feared I was changing into my aunts, these once wiry and tough women used to hard desert life fated to being beached in front of the television. But their nomadic instincts adapted to the situation and ended up manifesting themselves in new ways—for example, in the regular changing of interior decoration. It was seasonal: every few months everyone got together and traded their curtains and carpets to get the feeling of having a new room. Instead of a change in place, they ended up changing their wallpaper or zoning out with the TV on mute, satellite views of Mecca alternating with angles of the *Kaaba* from different surveillance cameras. Like the photorealistic tropical island on Faraj's door, there was something so melancholy about all these flattened, unattainable places and dreams and urges. They were filling the house with a sense of defeat. By the end of that summer, I was convinced that all the women in my family had forgotten what it was like to be fearless and what it had once meant to be free.

14

UPSILON SCORPII •
THE STING • اللسعة

Everything was changing, and I couldn't do anything to stop it. The house was hectic with preparations for Uncle Faraj's imminent wedding in Saudi, and very little of it had to do with the groom, who was sent on errands, mostly to the tailors or the *souq*. A photo of Amna, the bride-to-be, circulated around the house. She was fat but beautiful, or rather fat *and* beautiful, and everyone used the word *delouaa* to describe her, as though it were a good thing to be the human equivalent of veal—milk-fed and sheltered. I spent a lot of time staring at the picture, studying what set of attributes stacked up to make her such a prized beauty. She was five years older than me, cinched into a tight dress, body contorted to display her hair and ass and face all at once. Her makeup was extreme and caused her to look like a drag queen, a persistent look that is still the fashion in the Gulf.

I stood in front of the mirror in Falak's wardrobe and pulled my *jalabiya* in tight to reveal a bloated paunch, lopsided hips, and flat butt. Something terrible seemed to have happened to my body over the past two months in Doha. Rather than feeling the fabled sense of completion everyone kept promising womanhood would bring, I felt frantic and aimless, as though I'd lost something important. I became cranky and aggressive and paced the house, loitering in doorways and moaning in English about how bored I was. I pestered Tiny, the maid, while she made flatbread on a burner in the carport; I bothered Umi while she churned butter in her goatskin and Aunt Zayna while she pumped milk from her swollen breast to feed her baby. It was as though when Falak told me not to go there, she had drawn a line in the sand and dared me to cross it, and I always ended up back at the side door that led to the men's *majlis*. The *majlis* had begun to take on, for me, the expansive feeling of the "outside."

I peeked into the *majlis*. Aunt Moody's sons were playing Super Nintendo. I sized the three of them up. Like most boys from our family they were wiry, with sharp, beaky noses. I watched silently as the little one worked Sub-Zero up into decapitating Johnny Cage. I stepped in, lurking at the back of the *majlis*. AbdAllah was the most hostile, and the youngest seemed almost afraid. It was like walking into a bar and wanting a turn at the pool table. I shuffled up closer and sat behind them to watch. AbdAllah scooted away from me, then lost to Zayed when he took his eyes off the screen. I reached for the player B controls to get a turn. I took my place and blinged through the players. Of course, I chose Sonya Blade. Zayed eyed me sideways and waved his hand in front of his face like I stunk. His brothers egged him on as Sub-Zero and Sonya appeared on the screen. Thumbing a random combination of buttons I kicked his ass.

But rather than my getting to play the next round fair and

square, AbdAllah grabbed the controls out of my grip and backed away. He hoarded the game console up to his chest. "Okay, you played, now go back inside."

They weren't afraid of me, I knew. They were scared of what might happen if they got caught *with* me. All I wanted to do was play *Mortal* fucking *Kombat*.

"Give it to me!" I roared, and lurched for the controls.

The punchy synth intro kicked in and wound me up. If they just let me play out a K.O. I was going to resign in peace and return to my place in the women's quarters. But now the boys were positioned together like stormtroopers in the corner of the *majlis*. I turned, pretending I was going to leave, but instead locked the door behind me. *It was on*. Preparing for the showdown, they tied their *thobes* up around their waists, exposing their baggy long underwear and skinny ankles to give themselves room to kick. I tied my *jalabiya* up around my hips and took my best Sumo wrestling stance.

I plowed for the middle one, lifting him over my shoulder and tossing him over my back. Too stunned to do anything and afraid to touch me, AbdAllah went down in similar fashion before gathering himself enough to grab my hair and drag me onto the floor.

"That's it!" I growled, hysterical and frenzied from the contact.

I blindly grabbed for him and got his leg. Pulling myself up, I bit the only place I could reach: his ankle. Then he started howling for mercy. The handle of the living room door rattled, and then Aunt Moody burst through the door. We all froze, the battle of the sexes halted by the shadow of authority. It was a moment of mid-battle action captured forever in my mind like a war memorial, the younger two boys tugging at my legs, my teeth clamped around my cousin's ankle while he made like he was going to scalp me.

"Separate!" she commanded.

The other three let go and I dropped the leg out of my mouth like a stunned dog with a bone.

"What is *wrong* with you?!" she shrilled.

The boys blanched, and I turned bright red.

"Shameful! Shameful! Shameful!"

—was the only thing I understood from her tirade. I found myself being yanked by the neck of my *jalabiya* out the door and marched back to the women's quarters. When we got back in the house Aunt Moody honked my left boob to illustrate I was too old to be playing with boys.

"One of my sons might want to marry you someday—"

"Ew!" I grimaced.

"Do you want them to remember you like that?" she pressed, as though incest were a desirable outcome to this situation.

Yes! I thought to myself. I really wanted them to remember me as the one who could kick their asses.

After the skirmish in the *majlis*, Umi Safya came to the wise conclusion that I ought to get out of the house more. And so, having violated almost every expectation of a young woman of Al Dafira, I was banished from women's country to the passenger seat of my uncle Faraj's un-air-conditioned truck. Faraj had been nominated to be my caretaker. He had the right combination of free time (unemployment) and a ride. He did not, however, appreciate having to ferry me around town. I was an embarrassment to him as I slouched in the truck, scowling out the window, headphones over my *shala*, mouthing the lyrics to "Everybody Hurts" at a bus full of Filipino laborers.

Our communication barrier was deep. We had a mutually kept silence for the first week, and I had plenty of time to observe him while he drove from the post office to the Falcon Market to the paddock outside the city where Umi kept her goats. Aside from a brief peck on the cheek when he had picked me up at the airport, there had been no interaction between us. In addition to the stilted nature of our relationship, I found myself too grammatically challenged to address him. Having obtained all my knowledge of Arabic in the segregated classroom of my female family, I had never learned how to conjugate words in a masculine way. Faraj was equally uncommunicative with me, his English more nonexistent than my Arabic. And anyway, he seemed preoccupied with some secret business during our outings, pulling up off the road to check his pager, which everyone referred to as his "bleep." Often he'd urgently pull into gas stations where he'd hole up in a phone booth for half an hour talking cautiously into the phone, rolling a bottle of cola over his face to keep cool.

Being a twin, Faraj really was the male version of Falak. He had a carefully contrived personal style: a perpetual two-day growth of facial hair and a starched cobra-style *gutra* worn at a jaunty angle. The combination made him look rakish and cool. His truck was similar in character, a two-door Nissan Patrol jumped up on extra-high wheels with blue racing stripes and a decal that read *"Masha'Allah"* in the back window. Every morning I rode out with him while he ran errands for my aunts and Umi Safya. Although I'd felt trapped and bored in the house, I realized that being a woman also spared you from another kind of boredom. This became abundantly clear to me on occasions such as the seven hours Faraj spent waiting in line at the Ministry of Municipal Affairs while I got heatstroke in the truck. As the sun reached its zenith, I started hallucinating that the waves of roiling heat had started to float over the truck. I was so seasick and dehydrated by the time Faraj returned that I had to vomit. He held my *shala* back while I puked.

Like Falak and horror films, the one thing Faraj and were able to bond over was juice cocktails. The juice stalls were burrowed into the most unlikely places all over the city. By day the juice stall was an oasis of color in the drab tan of everyplace else. Plastic fruit festooned the windows, and signs die-cut to look like icicles promised relief from the heat. At night they turned into beacons of neon in otherwise dark residential neighborhoods, the garishly decorated interiors now fully visible through the shop-front windows. Our ritual on the way home every day was to pull up to Hot 'n' Cool Stall, where I'd read aloud from the menu, sounding out the transliterated letters of drinks like Tropical Storm, Year 2000, Land Cruiser, and Milky Banana. Faraj would honk like he was in rush-hour traffic until a pissed-off-looking Indian man slumped out to take our orders.

"One Rolex and one small Combyuter," Faraj ordered.

It didn't matter what we asked for, Mercedes or Kerala Kiss, they all came out in the same gloopy swirl of sunset colors in a soggy cardboard cup. Then we'd sit together in the truck, slushing the straws around inside our drinks and listening to classic Mohammed Abdu on the radio.

It was on one such pit stop, sucking down a smoothie, when he finally broke the ice. I was absorbed in loudly vacuuming the froth off the bottom of my cup when he blurted out, in Arabic, "Are you happy here?"

I slushed the juice with my straw, suspicious of this unexpected attempt at chitchat. "Sure," I answered. His question was loaded. I thought about how I felt freer here than I had in America. Plus there was more to look at, more to think about, even if there was less for me to do. "How are you?" I asked him.

He puffed his chest against the seatbelt and deflated in a sigh. "Not so good, *wella*, not so good." He shook his head. "One minute."

He held his finger up in front of me and produced a delicate envelope from somewhere in his *thobe*. He plucked a photo from it and laid it in the palm of my sticky hand. The image was of a girl, but it was most definitely *not* his fiancée, Amna. This girl was posed in front of a painted sky, her face was a perfect oval dented at the chin in a cute cleft, her nose was strong and hooked like a falcon, and her eyes were big and black. She wore lace gloves and her hands ramped under her face in what was meant to be a poetic pose of longing. *Why was he showing me this?* I wondered nervously, and handed the photo back to him.

"I need to see her before I get married," he explained. "But her father won't let her answer the phone." I knew what he was going to ask before he asked it. "Will you help?"

I'd already gotten in trouble twice this summer. The

worst thing I could do now was to be implicated in an affair. Faraj's bleeper bleeped, and he jumped with it. He started the car and turned to me. "Well?" he asked, eager for an answer. "Fine," I agreed grudgingly, and we drove off in a direction I hadn't been before.

My age and inexperience aside, it was becoming profoundly clear to me that love in the context of youth culture in Qatar was far more complex than anything I had ever seen on MTV. Because segregation between the sexes is so enforced, when a love affair does gain any kind of traction, like Faraj's did, it has to fly below the radar. As you can imagine, like anything forced to lurk in the shadows, love (which we know will always find a way) adapts and manifests itself in more subversive forms of expression. Falak had told me about *boyahs*, but they were only a small piece of the larger story.

"There she is," Faraj said reverently as we pulled up to an impressive mansion. His tone was hushed, as though he were witnessing some kind of natural wonder. I followed his finger to a dark rooftop across a busy road from where we sat in a gas-station parking lot.

"Where?" I tried to focus my eyes to find this magical creature.

"There! The pink thing!" he whispered.

I followed his eyes to a patch of color cut through by shadow. It could have been anything—a piece of laundry, a toy—but then it moved and I saw a projectile glint in the streetlamp and land in the sand bordering the outside wall of the house.

"Okay, go see what she threw!"

I slumped across the road to investigate, a little resentful at being treated like his hunting dog. I came to the spot; a heavy glass perfume bottle lay shattered in the dust, a vessel to deliver her message. I plucked a piece of paper out of the crater of glass shards and ran back across to where Faraj was waiting. "Call me in ten minutes," it read. "I'll be at the phone."

We loitered for ten minutes near a booth and then Faraj dialed a number, keeping his eye on the house the whole time. He seemed surprised to hear a man answer and handed me the phone. I said in my most grown-up voice, "Good evening, is Kholoud there? This is her English teacher calling."

Faraj grinned, pleased at how foreign and therefore official I sounded. I heard a shuffling and a woman's voice came softly across the line.

"Hello?" It came in a half-whisper.

Faraj yanked the phone out of my hand and breathed deeply into the phone. She kept the ruse up, responding as though he were her English teacher. A date and place were set for a rendezvous, and she pledged she'd be there no matter how elaborately she'd have to lie. So began my job as go-between for Faraj and Kholoud in the final days leading up to his marriage to Amna.

That night we cruised through Doha with the windows down, passing through Electricity Street on our way—a miniaturized version of Piccadilly Circus, where even the tiniest shop front boasted a massive bank of neon. All the signs were fairly abstract, like "Amira Services" and "Al-Maha Machinery." Signs like these flickered with epileptic intensity over otherwise unmarked doors. I remember in particular the outrageous promise of "World of Magic," which turned out to be a carpet wholesaler. We came out of the manic *souq* area and onto the corniche, the smooth rim of concrete that ran the length of the city from the port to the Sheraton still standing at the far end of the bay. Except for the young shoots of office towers now sprouting up around it, it was the same as I'd remembered it.

When we came to a red light I could see Faraj sifting through his English vocabulary for something to say, finally settling on "thank you."

I didn't know how to express the vicarious rush of freedom and happiness I was experiencing, so I just grinned at him.

Now that we were in cahoots, conversation flowed more naturally. He'd stop and start his cassette tapes and quiz me on Aline Khalaf lyrics: "Fire! Wind!" she crooned. "Heart! Ember!" I called back, proud of my new Arabic words. But Faraj wasn't being a teacher consciously; he just thought it was funny to hear me sing Aline Khalaf songs. Sometimes after that, he talked to me about how pent up and angry he was for not being able to marry outside the tribe. After my mother, one outsider married into the family had proved enough, so Faraj's hopes of marrying a non-Bedouin girl from the city were crushed. As it turned out, Faraj, the only man of the household, had had little choice in the matter.

All through August, I rode shotgun in the Patrol. Faraj offered small, helpful hints as to mistakes I was making. For example, he demonstrated for me how to walk in my *abaya* while giving the effect of floating just above the ground.

Even today I haven't mastered how to walk in a light, skimming motion to replace my cow-hocked trod. During my apprenticeship to Faraj, I learned the subtleties of courtship in Qatar and the ins and outs of phone dating before mobile phones. After a few weeks, I was able to pick up on the complex, subtle, and usually unsuccessful exchanges going on in public all the time. As we walked through the mall, boys slowed down and muttered their numbers at women, who on closer sight were old enough to be their mothers. Men slipped notes with their phone numbers into the open purses of girls drifting past. There was an intense energy of longing and desire that hung over the long strips of mall corridors, and it had nothing to do with what was displayed in the windows of the shops.

The night of the rendezvous with Kholoud came, and Faraj called me to his room. It was tiny and mostly filled with his bed, a twin-size cot. Above this hung a poster of the Emirati singer Ahlam. She smiled down on us maniacally, face masked with the painted-on joy of a circus clown. Cassette tapes littered the pillows at the head of the bed, and a tape player lay propped against the wall. There was no other furniture in the space, although the screen of a small television peered out of a wall of bedding the family stored for camping trips. At the top of this dam of polyester blankets and pillows he had placed a plastic tea tray and filled it with his prize possessions: bottles of *oud*, a pair of diamanté silver cuff links, a white leather slipcase for when he wanted to change the look of his bleep, and a pretty gilded Quran. It occurred to me then that Faraj, for all the comparative liberty he had, was still cloistered from the world, if in a different way than his sisters.

The meeting with Kholoud was set for Aladdin's Kingdom on Family Day, which was the only day her father would permit her to leave the house. Family Day is a Gulf institution in which once a week, every week, public spaces are inverted to become effectively private. Malls, beaches, and fun parks like Aladdin's Kingdom become female-only, a shift happens, and single men are not allowed in. Women use the opportunity to eat in the food courts, pelt the monkeys in the zoo with snack food, and lose their lunches on the Pirate Ship. The only way a male can enter the gates of one of these pop-up women's countries is as chaperone to a female family member. This is where I came in. Alone, Faraj could not pass security at the smoking oil lamp marking the entrance to Aladdin's Kingdom; with me in tow it would be easy.

After we'd been waved in with a larger crowd of children and nannies, we looked for a place to wait. The air was heavy with popcorn dust and burnt sugar. Faraj walked cautiously down the path, sweat like dew on the bristles of his upper lip. He obviously felt like a trespasser, a stranger, maybe even a criminal. We found a bench alongside the perimeter fence of the amusement park and watched the Zipper swing and the Tea Cups plunge and spin women and children. It was eerily quiet on the outskirts of the park, carnival music drowned out by the heavy creak of pivoting metal. Faraj was too nervous to look around much, so I had to keep a lookout for the signal Kholoud had promised us. We waited almost an hour before it came, and only I saw her.

At least I *hoped* it was Kholoud who led us to the Gravitron, a squat, UFO-type ride that used centrifugal force to pin you to sliding slats of pleather. It was full of kids, so we weren't able to make our way over to where Kholoud and her friends were. They were holding hands silently, watching Faraj and me. As the ride started up, the force suctioned their veils to their faces and their *abaya*s to their bodies. Faraj strained to turn his head away from the alluring sight but he was just as pinned back, his white *gutra* sucked against the wall like wet toilet paper. The hint of Kholoud's body through thin black rayon, outlined in flickering Gravitron light, was lurid. Her *niqab* was folded up to her eyes and revealed a perfect hot-pink pout glistening with lip gloss. She blindly tried to pull it back down over her face, but it was too late and, anyway, she was smiling. Swept up in the melodrama playing out before me, I felt a swell of pity for my immobilized uncle, days away from marrying a girl he didn't love.

Faraj and I tottered out ahead of Kholoud, unsure of our footing on the metal ramp. Faraj herded me to the outer edge of the Gravitron, where no one could see us. He stuffed something into my hand and said, "When she comes out, give this to her." He looked around anxiously and then backed off a ways and tried to look casual near a garbage can. I stood at the end of the corral waiting for Kholoud to emerge, so caught up in the drama that I started to pit out through my *abaya*. She and her friends exited the ride last and zigzagged through the fence toward me. As she approached, she held her hand out, palm up, for me to deliver the gift. She was obviously familiar with this trick. One of her friends put her hand on my shoulder and drew me into a stroll away from Faraj while Kholoud read the note without breaking stride.

Kholoud came to the end of the note and addressed me, her voice warbled with a sob. "Tell your uncle I hate him," she declared. Then she ripped his note into pieces, all the while looking over my shoulder directly at Faraj. He was standing at the garbage can, looking like he might cry. The girl holding my shoulder released me and I was left to drift in their wake, as confused at her reaction to my uncle's farewell note as he was. I went back to Faraj and we sat together on the bench, watching the scraps of his love letter as they were swept up with the litter of candy wrappers and cans of Shani.

15

MU DRACONIS • THE DANCER •
الراقص

The road to Saudi was a bleak memento mori marked every few kilometers by the twisted husks of crashed cars. We were on our way to Al-Hasa in Saudi Arabia, where Faraj's bride awaited him and the wedding, and I was looking forward to seeing Baba again before catching my flight home. We were crowded into Faraj's Nissan Patrol and through the *berga* covering my face, I couldn't see where I ended and the other girls started, for all the black fabric we were draped in. To make the journey even more uncomfortable, the A/C was still broken. So with the windows down and our *abaya*s aloft in the wind, we approached the Saudi border like a bat with a great flapping wingspan of rayon and polyester.

More than a week had passed since the rendezvous with Kholoud and her message of rejection. After that, Faraj had seemed to gentle down as the marriage grew near, and was now fully resigned to his fate. He seemed almost relieved. As much as the rules of the tribe were a snare he was tangled up in, they were also a safety net for when decisions were too difficult to make. Now, with the wedding only days away, the whole clan had begun to converge on Al-Hasa.

They came en masse down Salwa road, past the U.S. Air Force base and onward in a caravan of trucks. It reminded me of traveling in the Suburban full of kids out to Saudi when Dima and I were little. The pileup at the border was mostly other relatives, or so it seemed as Faraj made rounds with the car, honking, waving, and revving the overheating engine at cars full of people. He pulled up alongside a small trailer with an image of a woman in a *berga* painted onto the flapping door. I tumbled out with the rest and waited while Faraj doled our passports out of a stack, checking the photos and then holding them out to us without even checking to see who was who. His skill at telling us apart even with our faces covered was impressive.

Inside the trailer, an overweight woman reclined on pillows on the floor next to a radio. Irritated at the interruption, she got up and received the jumble of our passports all at once. She flipped through the pages, yawning with boredom, and scanned the photos, calling our names out individually.

"Falak!" she barked. Falak lifted her veil for the woman to compare to the photo. She roughly stamped the passport and called my name out. "Safya!" I lifted my *berga* for her to compare my face. She squinted at me, then looked down at the photo. She shook her head forbiddingly. "Why does it say here born in USA?"

I grunted, not wanting my accent to give me away and looked in panic to Falak for help.

Luckily a line had started to form behind me, so the woman reluctantly stamped my passport and let us go.

I hung close to Falak as we walked through the border to

the other side, where Faraj was waiting with the car. Dogs were barking in a kennel somewhere, and I glared out of my veil into the two-way mirrors that reflected the checkpoint booths as we passed. Far from finding it oppressive, I discovered that wearing a *berga* over my face was actually kind of fun. This was before *berga* became such a hot-button issue in the West, and wearing it was in no way political to me. Instead it was like undergoing an easy transformation into a bona fide Al-Dafira woman, anonymous, invisible, and with the sun and sand protection over my face: invincible. I felt as though I could go anywhere and, out of politeness, no one would bother me.

We came to the other side of the customs pavilion, where border guards pulled up the upholstery and rifled through the glove compartment of Faraj's truck. Several small cabins with palm trees were clustered at one end of the border, laundry hung out to dry on lines strung across the back of trucks.

"People live here?" I asked Falak.

She looked around and shrugged. "Probably people who get sick or have the wrong papers stay there."

There was something so pleasing about these prefab homes in no-man's-land. As we crossed the border and headed northwest to Al-Hasa, I fantasized about being stranded back there at the border. How it would be to have my own little cabin with a palm tree in front, hemmed in tightly to these few stateless kilometers between the Qatari and Saudi borders, where the land belonged as much to me as to anyone else.

Al-Hasa was an oasis town where the famous Friday

market used to draw Al-Dafira from all directions. We'd come a few days early to find cheap dresses for the wedding, and there were droves of deal-seeking Qataris just like us who came to Saudi to buy dates and clothes and jewelry and perfumes with strangely translated Chinese names like *Accidentally Wildly Jealous* for a few riyals less than they were priced in Doha.

Faraj drove us directly to the part of the *souq* where the *abayas* were cheap and the party dresses hot messes. The garments chosen by my aunts for Faraj's wedding were all froths of lace with huge drumstick-style sleeves. They each took turns in the tiny shop, trying on gowns more bedazzled than a Las Vegas showgirl's costume. A mannequin stood at the center of the tiny room, her head removed but her fiberglass body bolted to the platform. The details of her body were barely hinted at with softly molded indentations, and she sported a beaded Spandex tunic that quit mid-thigh and rained glass droplets down to her toes.

Aunt Moody emerged from the little changing booth in a spumescent mint-green number that came with a bag of matching accessories, including ribbon rosettes, colored contacts, and a vial of green glitter with which to dust her cleavage and hair if extra glam were required. "Safya! Aren't you going to try anything on?" she asked.

By this point I was so sweaty and tired and twisted up in my *abaya* that the thought of trying on a tulle-and-sequin dress was about as appealing as getting tarred and feathered. I shook my head and sat on the sidelines until decisions had been made about the gowns and we headed to a relative's house, where I collapsed onto the cushions and wondered dozily where Baba was and when he was going to turn up. He'd promised at the airport in Abu Dhabi that he'd be here. Where was he? Had he heard about my brawl with the cousins? Was he upset with me?

These questions were still swirling in my head when Aunt Moody interrupted my brooding. "Safya, you have to look your best! Everyone is expecting you to dance. They haven't seen you since you were small."

I suppose this was her way of making peace, but I was hesitant to dance after my birthday incident.

"Your father will be proud if he knows his daughter danced."

Moody really knew how to get at my underbelly. The next thing I knew I was on my feet being led around the room in an impromptu dance lesson. The elderly women all clapped in time with music from the television as Moody tied a *shala* around my hips so they could all assess my lumpen figure. She then made me clod-hop in time with her on the balls of my feet. Someone produced a dress for me to try on. It was ill-fitting and looked like the kind of confection a Bavarian princess might wear, all sky blue with puffed sleeves and a huge skirt tiered with ribbons. Moody paraded me to the middle of the room, where she left me standing in front of everyone, looking and feeling like a fairy-tale reject. I twisted slowly at the center of the carpet for everyone to have a look before they decided collectively, "It's perfect!" *This*, they decided, would be my gown.

The day before Faraj's wedding, squeals of pain ripped

through the house. A shrill howl of "*M-Hagg-Sanaa*!" came from the bedroom.

"What's going on?" I asked. The door to the bride's room was locked.

More whimpering came from the other side of the door. "The *halawa* lady has arrived," Falak replied ominously, and I sensed the slightest hint of sadistic glee in her eye.

Halawa, I would soon discover, was a kind of depilatory that not only rips hair out but removes a whole layer of skin. The *halawa* itself is a golden glop of boiled sugar, water, and lemon the consistency of thick honey. We all waited in the living room while the henna lady drew patterns on the hands and feet of my cousins. There were different styles of henna: North African henna looked like fish bones, Indian was all peacocks and paisley, Sudani was black dye in thick stripes, and Gulfi consisted of dots and florals.

Aunt Moody brought a canister of kerosene to mix with the green paste. "It'll make the henna *nice* and dark!" she claimed.

My turn came, and the henna lady suggested I try the newest *moda*—a sort of tribal-tattoo-style swirl placed like ass antlers on the lower back. Although my taste in fashion was dubious, I couldn't keep up with early '90s global trashiness and asked for regular old hands and feet. A few seconds after contact with my skin, the design started to burn itself into my flesh. Despite the pain, Moody was right; the kerosene did indeed give the henna a pleasing dark burgundy color. The bride emerged from her room a hairless wonder. Everyone crowded around to feel how soft her arms and legs were while the henna lady laid out newspaper and then laid

Amna out on it flat. She got the whole deal: head and shoulders, knees and toes. The henna looked like an invasive ivy, crowding up from her ankles to her thighs.

Like everything else, the wedding was segregated into female and male receptions: two canvas tents were pitched beside each other on the road in front of the house. There was a catwalk-style dais at the center; swans and roses and a great big moon hung from the tent poles. Some of my cousins were snooty about the tents. Compared to the air-conditioned halls of hotels in Doha, this was straight ghetto. As was being roughly frisked for cameras by two stern security women at the entrance to the tent. They wore police caps pinned on top of their *hijabs*. The tent was full of freshly done-up usually veiled women in fringe miniskirts and braless chiffon numbers, which is why the only cameras allowed inside were those of the "professional ladies' photographers"—mostly Filipino women armed with ostentatious SLR cameras. They posed girls into demented glamour-shot poses that would then be traded among friends as mementos.

Immediately upon our entry a row of girls gathered for kisses. I felt like a pigeon bobbing my head in and out, cheek to cheek, coming to the end of the line with a greasy smear of rouge and powder on the right side of my face. Making my way to the end of this lineup, I saw Flu having her portrait taken with my younger sisters, pinky finger under chin, head cocked in an absurd cutesy pose.

"Safya! We're taking a photo for your baba! Come sit with us!" she called to me.

I wandered reluctantly over and hung near the edge of the

frame. The photographer shoved me in front of the back-drop, which was supposed to be some kind of Alpine location and reminded me of Mount Rainier in the spring. We all sat there together frozen at various beauty angles waiting for the photo to be taken.

"I'm so proud of you! Look! You're like a real Al-Dafira girl now!" Flu said as she squeezed my shoulders and kissed my cheek. "Your baba will be proud to see you all grown up like this!"

I smiled as faintly as possible, worried the crust of makeup clinging to my face might crack.

We were served cellophane-wrapped wedding favors—shriveled pistachios and sugared almonds in nougat. The dinner included a whole baby lamb splayed out over a hill of rice. The lamb still had its eyes. Out of its back rose a tier of trays with condiments: yogurt, pickles, pepper, salt. The meat was butter-soft; I tore off pieces with my hands. But it wasn't until after dinner that the main event began. The stage in the middle of the tent filled up with dancing girls all decked out in vibrant violet, shimmery mustard gold, and all different rainbow brights. Flesh burst the seams of silk dresses and the party burst the canvas tent, barely shielding the celebration from the bored male relatives who idled outside the tent in their cars. Nervous virgins and divorcées took their places on a catwalk that was auction house, runway, and dance floor all at once. Black-robed mothers of marriageable sons moved close in anticipation. Each eligible girl clambered onto the stage and was announced by the Sudanese wedding singers, called *daghagat*. They played drums and sang into battered microphones, feedback issuing from the cheap speakers. All the songs sounded the same to me, yet the girls all had their favorites.

A whisper flew low over the room that the men were coming, and in seconds, all the colors turned to black as the entire party grabbed for cover under whatever *abaya* they could find. I soon found that I was the only person still uncovered, and skittered from one cluster of black to another looking for shelter before finally ducking under a table near the bride's end of the dais. I peeked out through the lace tablecloth as the lights dimmed and the drumming began. I hoped this might be my chance to spot Baba, but the only familiar face belonged to Faraj, who appeared in a spotlight at the entrance to the tent. He was flanked by the bride's brothers, who cantered at his sides. He had groomed his beard into a perfect *saksuka* that looked to me like a soda-can tab stamped around his mouth. One of Amna's brothers raised a sword over his head and swung it around as the group of them proceeded to where the bride was perched, huge dress taking up most of the love seat. The fear on her chubby face was disguised at a distance by a protective layer of makeup, but from up close where I hid under the table it was clear she was petrified.

The newly amalgamated family now danced around the newlyweds together; Aunt Moody, wearing her *berga* over her face but with her braids exposed, was throwing riyal notes over their heads, the A/C scattering them in the air for the drummer ladies to hoover up. As Faraj led his new bride out the door, the band started up again, this time louder than before. Faraj's eyes were downcast and his face was shadowed. This was only the beginning of his recovery from losing Kholoud. I wished he'd look in my direction so I could give him a reassuring smile. But he didn't. I saw Aunt Moody coercing one of the musicians with a ten-riyal note. My stomach churned as I realized what she was doing. Sure enough, "Safya Matar!" they called into the crackling microphone. "Dance! Come on! Get up and shake it, girls!" they yelled in encouragement to the tent-flap flowers lurking along the edges of the room, avoiding the dance.

The Bene Gesserit litany from *Dune* buzzed in my ear: "Fear is the mind killer." The beat got going as I stepped up onto the platform to take my plunge, and I shambled up into a fast trot. My body wouldn't fall into sync with the rhythm; instead I kept tripping up on the sea of taffeta falling from my waistline. I felt the prickle of a hundred eyes burning my cheeks and told myself it was only in my head, no one was paying any attention to me. A mob of little girls skittered up with me and danced around my knees, whipping their hair around. I wanted to melt through the floor and disappear by the time I'd made two equitations around the floor. An overexcited elderly woman in front squawked in a hoarse voice, "Oh, boy! That American girl is dancing!" which caused the attention of the whole tent to focus on me.

This was too much. I plowed through the siege of little girls and half tumbled down to where Flu and Falak and the rest were shooing me to go back up. Ducking their pushy encouragement, I fished my *abaya* out of a pile in the corner, bundled up in black, and trudged off in the direction of the house we were staying in, hoping someone there might know where my father was.

A car flicked its brights at me. I ignored it. It honked, and a man yelled, "Sophie!" It was Baba. "So you danced?" he poked as I came to his window. There was a laugh suspended in his question. How did he know already?

"Can we go now?"

"Sure," he said, and turned the car around to drive me back to Abu Dhabi.

I changed into my American clothes under my *abaya*, and a few hours later we'd made it to the airport. Baba checked me in and handed me the mini photo album Flu and I had posed for. "You look very pretty here, like a real Al-Dafira girl."

The compliment faded when I saw the photo he was referring to. I sat in a heart-shaped cutout and my face had been masked by a romantic Gaussian blur to disguise the acne.

"I'm glad you like it," I answered, and handed it back to him.

"I'll keep this one with me," he said, and folded it in half and slipped it into his wallet beside a photo I'd never seen of Ma alone in the Space Needle, backlit by the huge cockpit window of the revolving restaurant. "Tell your mama and sister I love them too much," he said before he left me at immigration.

"I will," I promised.

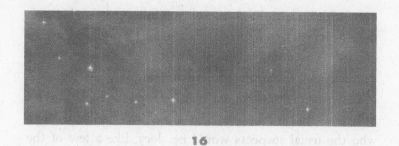

16

ETA BOÖTIS •
THE SOLITARY ONE • الفرد

On entering seventh grade, I found that everyone in my class had gone from gravel wars on the playground to groping behind the vending machines. My perception of boy-girl mixing had been blown way out of proportion by the deep sexual segregation of my time in Doha. But this new state of affairs was more mysterious to me than the euphemized "sexual intercourse" or the "special changes" happening to my body. I overheard talk of tonsil hockey, blow jobs, and finger-banging—all slang that was both nonspecific and evocative enough for me to be certain it was exciting. Every other hall break there were rats yelling "PDA!" at people holding hands, playing footsie, or even sharing cans of soda.

But looming larger than the sudden flurry of saliva swap meets was another big change. As is the custom in American schools, the class had begun to coagulate into groups typified not only by the John Hughes hierarchy of jocks, geeks, and freaks, but very clearly by race. The Mexican kids, the Samoans, and the new Russians banded together into their respective groups, and then there were the Native American kids, who hung around in the area but were divided into their own private school near the casino. I'd jumped the trap of needing to belong to my tribe in Qatar, but now there was a new kind of tribalism to figure out: middle-school cliques.

Between a gutter punk named Joey and the Mexican kids in Dickies and wifebeaters, the school had already decided who the usual suspects would be. Joey, like a few of the other poorer kids, had to do cafeteria duty to pay for his lunches.

Of course, this will lead anyone to become a target, and it all rose to a crescendo one afternoon while Joey was wiping down tables. Kane, one of the junior varsity football players, crossed him somehow. It was unclear how the fight started. Some claimed Kane had called Joey a nigger, but it really didn't matter what he'd done, because Joey's reaction was fierce. He whipped Kane across the face with his disinfectant-soaked rag and brought the huge cafeteria table crashing down on Kane's back. In some tellings Joey had flipped Kane off; in others, Kane had spit in Joey's face. Whatever the truth was, it became an inflamed brawl of more than twenty boys swinging at each other with no apparent goal beyond having a rumble. It spilled out of the cafeteria into the courtyard, and then from the courtyard onto the street. Girls tried to pull their boyfriends out of the struggling tangle of testosterone, terrified of having no one to make out with if they got suspended. The science teacher, Mr. Heddon, got elbowed in the face and ended up in the nurse's office before anyone else did. The only thing everyone seemed to agree on was that *obviously* the fight had happened because Joey was black, or at least half black, and anyway, aside from Nevaeh Ripley, he was the only black person in the school and so a very easy target.

When Kane returned to school from suspension and Joey didn't, a rumor spread that he had skipped town and gone to ride the rails up and down the West Coast. One of the dropout girls from the park spread a rumor in reverent tones about how Joey had gone to Los Angeles to meet his hardcore heroes. I thought about him every time I sat in the cafeteria, muddy footprints on the floor, backpacks slung on the backs of chairs, expanding areolae of grease saturating my paper plate full of seventy-five-cent tater tots. It was all too depressing. I began to obsess about Joey and placed him at the center of my own private tall tale, in which he rode on top of a Burlington Northern freight car all the way to L.A. I added him to my pantheon of heroes—partly for being a mongrel like me and partly just for managing to get out of this little town.

It was during this time, while school and home seemed to be falling apart around me, that I became particularly interested in dystopias. I preferred the classics, which says more about me being a pretentious fifteen-year-old than that I had any discerning taste: *Brave New World*, *The Gates to Women's Country*, *1984*, *A Handmaid's Tale*, and my predictable favorite, *A Clockwork Orange*. I rarely ever lingered in the sci-fi/fantasy wing of the library anymore, although I still snuck listens to *Ziggy*, now on CD. I got my sci-fi kicks by searching for *X-Files* fanfic on the Internet during the coming years' still lonesome and miserable lunch hours and filling floppy discs full of Fox Mulder JPEGs, Battle Angel GIFs, and tinny, MIDI-fied versions of "Diamond Dogs."

I lobbied to get the Internet at home, but the Internet cost money, and although Ma had a temp job at the time, things were tight. So the day after I turned sixteen I went to the cineplex across the river (the same place Ma and Baba used to put me to sleep during *Close Encounters*) and asked for a job. Just like Gramma's farm, the cineplex had been in the wake of a bad slump ever since people started selling off valley property and migrating to cheap housing developments in the surrounding hills. At the time I was born, it had been in a prime location on the valley's main drag; now it was all used-car dealerships and dollar stores. The cinema's main clientele consisted of napping winos and twelve-year-old boys who knew the theater was so desperate for customers they could get in to see R-rated movies without ID.

My job was to sit in the box office and listen to the wind on the busted nozzle of the mic as it swept over the empty parking lot. Even on days I didn't have to go in to work, I pretended I did. I'd settle in for my ninth viewing of *The Fifth Element*, letting the pre-movie intro (at Regal Cinemas it was a "cosmic roller coaster") take me away over icy cups of Pepsi and giant corn kernel explosions. Every night when the last show got out, I'd shut off all the lights but the soft gold glow of the popcorn machines and go through my final tasks of scouring the soda fountain, emptying the butter vats, and running the old roto-sweeper over the huge lobby carpet. I dreaded having to leave that theater and went into a sort of rock-garden Zen, scooting from one end of the galaxy-patterned rug to the other. At 11:30 sharp Ma would pull up to the lobby, signal with her brights through the bank of glass doors, and then wait in the darkness for me to come out. It was less than a mile away, and yet she always refused to let me walk because I had to cross the river. When we got home, more often than not, we'd find Gramma all dressed up with no place to go or conversing with people who weren't alive anymore.

As Gramma began to prefer the company of ghosts to the living, Ma decided the time had come to move her into a home. This change came in the spring of my sophomore year. Dementia had been setting in for a long time and had already siphoned off most of her memory, including the ones of Dima and me. It was subtle at first, a puncture somewhere in the membrane between the past and the present; a name would slip, or sometimes whole conversations would leak out from other times and other places. The disease was infiltrating all of our lives and had begun to partition her days. I became accustomed to her thinking I was her long-dead sister, "Sis," and that I worked at the race course, which she regularly begged us to take her to "for a little gamble."

After winter break Ma sold the farm to pay for Gramma's care, adding our patch of open earth (one of the last swatches of dirt in the area) to the belt of concrete that had filled the valley. A surveyor came with a compass, prism, tripod, and ranging rod. He outlined the property in his book. The man who owned the trailer park made an offer to take all our acreage and the house, all the way up to the shaggy riverbank. He gave us two weeks to clear out the house and leave. After the deal, Ma calculated how much there was, "enough for about six years in a nice place." Each acre would pay for approximately a year of medicine, a room in a nursing home, daily portions of boxed mashed potatoes, and prune juice.

It was a difficult decision to make, because the money raised from selling the farm would not guarantee that Gramma's memory would ever return. Every day after school and before work I went to visit Gramma. The home was called Logan Grove—an almost maniacally benign-sounding name for such a deeply strange place. The place had been built as an Escher-esque warren designed specifically to allow residents with cognitive problems to wander smoothly through the day without being reminded they were trapped. There were hallways that doubled back, doors that led to nowhere, and one-way mirrors all over the place. Being a teenager in the halls of Logan Grove was like being on a badly hemmed version of *The Truman Show*. Kitchens bled into nursing stations, candy stripers were instructed to play along with residents' delusions, and there were even a few tabby cats that provided cuddles to the wheelchair-bound. The lobby was the creepiest part of all. It was trussed up to resemble a small town square. It had a working beauty salon and a trompe l'oeil bank, and at the center of this no-horse town stood a large chess table—an apt choice for the centerpiece to this sad, still life.

Ever since Gramma had been put in the home, she had predictably become obsessed with returning to the home she'd been taken from. One afternoon around May she asked me for an unusually lucid favor, considering she usually hassled me for a trip to the races.

"The lilac bushes'll be blooming now, Sophia. You wanna go out in the back and bring some in for me?" It caught me by surprise, and she had used my real name. I had to do it for her.

Heading down the balding path to the bridge, I was

determined to get her a cutting from the lilac bush for her gloomy little room in Logan Grove. The old way to her house on foot had grown a comb-over of blackberry brambles, and the vines sent thorny trip wires across the path. I'd have to take the railway trestle. As I climbed up onto the thick wood timbers, the wet smell of river silt and pinecone wafted up in the air. The banks looked sore from surveyors tramping up and down, and for the first time I felt apprehensive of what I might find down there. The river swirled greenish brown several meters under me as I kept inching my way along. A way down on the trail I saw a figure all in black and thought for a moment about turning back. After all, the river was the *last* place I was supposed to be. The body was hunched with a hood, smoking a cigarette under a crab apple tree. It took me a moment before I recognized the configuration of hoodie, glasses, and posture: it was Joey.

"How'd you get up there?" he yelled at me from his spot on the ground.

I pointed toward the nursing home as I made it the last stretch of the bridge and jumped down onto the bank.

He threw out the stub he was smoking and took his hood down. "Want a smoke?"

We found a dryish plywood plank and laid it across the roots of the tree. It cracked in half under our combined weight. Joey was wearing black Converse duct-taped shut at the toe. His pants were sewn up with dental floss and covered with hardcore patches. His hoodie was covered in stitched-in anarchy signs, his hair was in a grown-out

Frohawk, and he was really, really dirty. The only snippet of incongruity in Joey's look was the fact that he was wearing thick-as-Coke-bottle glasses.

He rummaged through his worn-out leather-bottomed Jansport; it was covered in white-out scribbles. One said "Tara" and had a pair of boobs next to it; under that there was an ass with "Nicky" written in glitter pen. I knew who the girls were. They hung around the park. Tara was skinny with a shaved head like Tank Girl, and Nicky had all kinds of face piercings. He pulled a pack of Pall Malls out and lit one off a floppy clip of matches. It was the last light. I was nervous. I couldn't get my cigarette going because of the rain, so he lit mine off the end of his. I'd never seen anyone do that before.

"So what happened after that big fight?" I asked dumbly and hacked on my first puff.

"Which fight?" He inhaled deep.

It hadn't occurred to me until now that maybe Joey fought all the time; maybe the fight I'd witnessed was only one in a real-world life of fighting Joey led. I felt stupid and fell silent. He dug his heels into the ashy leaves. They hadn't finished rotting from the fall before. Rain was really starting to pour now and the river a few yards from us was unusually green. He rubbed raindrops off his glasses with the back of his sleeve.

"Well, where did you go?" I asked. "I mean, after you got suspended from school?"

Joey was peeling up the edge of the "hum" part of his Subhumans patch. "I went all over the place."

The rain slowed down, breaking into a rhythmless patter.

Joey got up and wandered toward the railroad trestle, where several shopping carts lay under the bridge. He squatted by the riverbank, a massive Crass circled-cross-with-a-line-through-it logo stretching across his back. A few timber trucks rumbled by over the bridge toward the freeway. I watched him rock back and forth on his haunches. Head down. Then I noticed the silver glint of a pot shoved under the blackberry brambles. A little clearing a way back had a sleeping bag, and alongside the spot where I sat was the burnt-out circle of a fire pit. I began to piece together the gloomy truth that Joey had probably never left Puyallup at all that year. He hadn't gone to California; he had been living rough out here. I shuddered and remembered my lilac promise to Gramma.

"I better get going," I said, and stamped out my half-smoked cigarette under a pile of mulch.

After that I wiped my palms off on my jeans and carried on up the riverbank toward the farm on a cloud of smoke and a hazy inkling that I should run away from this town, and soon. I walked the rest of the way up past the cotton-woods to the edge of our old property. What I saw when I reached the top of the path almost brought me to my knees. The fields were all plowed up. Orange plastic flags marked off different areas for laying concrete. The once neat berry tines were now piles of wooden post and wire. The lilac bush Ma and Baba had been married by, the cherry tree, and hundred-year-old firs were all toppled and mashed into the dirt by bulldozer treads. But the worst sight of all was the house, or, more specifically, the place where it had once been, now an open patch in the fields like a gashed-in crop circle of rubble. None of us had anticipated that the new owner would knock our home down.

I picked my way up to the open basement foundation, a big hole where the house should be. The uneven ground on the bottom was covered with mangled black plastic and held down with rocks. All the remains of the house had already been taken away, so it felt as if the house had just been beamed up, leaving a cement-block outline like chalk around a corpse. I kicked some broken glass into the hole. The place we called home had been erased right out from under us.

After that, the idea of leaving Puyallup grew beyond a hint of a thought into a full-on escape plan. Things seemed more vivid as I prepared to make my announcement. It was as if the forces behind every object and action were suddenly drumming up their energies double-time, shining brighter, like when clouds break and suddenly whatever it is you're looking at becomes more brilliant. That is how seeing that ripped-up land galvanized my resolve to go. I never saw Joey again, and I never heard Gramma call me by my real name after that. But the experience made me realize that the only way to become the person I wanted to be was to remove myself from the people who thought they knew me.

17

LAMBDA URSAE MAJORIS •
THE SECOND LEAP • القفزة الثّانية

Baba was eager to have me return to Doha, live with the family, and learn about Islam. Ma, on the other hand, wigged out when I told her I was leaving. We spent the remainder of our time together in mortal mother-daughter emotional combat.

"You had no trouble tossing me into the pool when I was a baby!" I screamed at her. "Why can't you let me go now?"

In response to this she would bring Dima into it, accusing me of abandonment. I felt bad enough about leaving Dima behind in that crappy little duplex without Ma rubbing it in. Still, the urge to leave had become more powerful than even my worst guilt. I officially withdrew from school in Puyallup and packed my suitcase several pounds overweight with a full stock of Dover Thrift Editions and my CD binder to keep me company. At the airport, Dima came inside to see me off, while Ma, out of protest, stayed in the car. My little sister and I hugged, knowing we would be apart a long time, then exchanged quick "okay, whatever, bye"s, and I was on my way. To what, exactly, I couldn't have guessed.

When I made it to Doha, I took my papers to the American

school, hoping my credits would transfer, and enrolled myself. Getting a place in the school was so competitive it was almost impossible for Qataris whose parents didn't work in the oil industry. After a very long afternoon in the principal's office explaining my story, it was decided, with some trepidation, that I should be granted a place in the junior class and that the usual payment of tuition up front would be waived for us to sort out later.

Baba gave me five hundred riyals to clothe myself for school. Falak took me to Souq Al-Jaber, where apparently all the trendy girls got their uniform fabric. She enlightened me as to various tricks, fashions, and rules as we browsed the stalls filled with reams of colorful prints and weaves.

"In high school you wear *long* skirts and white shirts," Falak said meaningfully as we looked at the tailor's spiral notebook full of ballpoint variations on the long-skirt design.

"So?" I said, flipping through the pleated, seamed, and mermaid patterns.

"You can't wear those." She gestured at the ragged hem of my jeans poking out from under my *abaya*.

I looked down at the dirty denim sticking out like a rat's tail. I got the hint.

We bought several meters of black and blue and maroon cotton for my skirts, and the tailor bashfully measured me over my *abaya*. Next we went to Sana and Splash (pronounced "Suhblash") for shirts and *accesswarat* like barrettes and plastic bracelets. As a gift, Falak furnished me with an array of *boofs*—these were just glorified hair clips handy for keeping *shalas* on. They were designed to give the illusion (and allure) of bounteous piles of thick, healthy hair underneath the veil. Basically the large hair clips of flowers and feathers were the female equivalent of a pair of socks masquerading as a bulge in a guy's trousers.

By the end of our shopping spree, my *abaya* was dredged in dust and the *shala* wasn't much better for wear, sliding off my head into a silky noose around my neck. My makeover was almost complete, except for one thing: after the tailor's fee we didn't have enough money for a new *abaya*. Falak promised to let me borrow some of hers until *Eid*, when my father would give me more money.

Falak's room back in Umi Safya's house was well-loved and cozy. During the day it was left open so it was a playroom for my many young cousins, and at night my two pregnant aunts slept on roll-out mats while Falak and I used the bunk. The night before school I was surprised to enter our bedroom to find a small desk in the corner of the room and a little stationery set waiting for me. On it was a note from Falak that simply read "good luck" in Arabic. I sat at the little desk area of my own and fondled my new pens and sniffed the pages of my fresh notebook, and then locked it all away in the one drawer under the desk that secured with a little key. I fell asleep that night to the naive hope that *tomorrow* was going to be the start of something new, with no shame, no guilt, and no mistakes in it.

A lot had happened since I'd been away. Faraj's marriage had lasted all of three weeks before Amna asked for a divorce. He had moved back in with Umi (some male-pattern uselessness is universal) and gotten a job as a night security guard. Because of his graveyard shift, Faraj was usually available to drive me to and from my new school. On the first day the old truck announced our arrival with a horrible black emission and a sputtering cough. The engine gargled as we coasted past the red, white, and blue gates, and then Faraj idled it to a crawl in front of my new classmates. They were a lot of good-looking, Bijan-clad senior boys leaning against their Jaguars and Land Rovers. The girls were all beautiful and looked grown-up, their clothes fresh off the backs of mall mannequins.

I started to wish I had something other than a public school uniform on under my *abaya*. They were all so well-adjusted and pleasingly *diverse* compared to Puyallup. It was like *90210* if it were acted entirely with international exchange students cast by Benetton. They came from India, Norway, Sudan, and Colombia, the offspring of ambassadors and oil barons. But the weirdly utopian assortment of cultures had boiled down into a patty-melt pastiche of an America I knew from experience didn't exist offscreen.

The truck groaned and settled down on its wheels with a cough just as we pulled up in front of a troupe of very classy-looking Qatari girls.

"You've *got* to be kidding me," I said aloud, echoing every teen sitcom I'd ever seen.

Some of the girls were in *abaya* and some were out. They looked down their noses at the Suburban through their D&G sunglasses. "Who are *they?*" Faraj asked as the girls backed away into the foyer and out of sight. His presence seemed to have spooked them. I slid low in my seat to avoid attracting any more attention, but Faraj was glam-blasted. "They look, they look . . . like angels!" he murmured like a fever-stricken madman.

Umi Safya's house, Madinat Al-Dafira, was just a few miles away from the school, and until this morning Faraj had been completely oblivious to the fact that this unreal enclave of Americana plucked from a different, imaginary TV world existed so close by.

I slid out the car door, shutting it quietly and hoping against hope that I'd remain unnoticed in my ill-fitting borrowed *abaya* and non-*marka*, or luxury brand, bag.

Although the characters were all different, the stage was set the same. The school seemed so excessively unreal I half expected the front to be a painted plank façade. I was surprised to enter and find that the illusion of an all-American high school didn't only continue inside the building, but became more intense. The halls were stacked with steel lockers, the same make as the ones in Puyallup; the floor was the same speckled linoleum; and with the A/Cs it had the same slightly frigid but stale breeze running throughout. I recognized the biology textbooks stacked beside the entrance to one of the classrooms. A bulletin board by the principal's office was lined with enthusiastic sayings and purple paper letters that shouted in all caps, "SHOOT FOR THE STARS, SENIORS!"

The Qatari girls who'd given Faraj and me the nasty looks approached me in the hall. The shortest one had deeply kohled eyes and a nose ring.

"Hey, I'm Noor. This is Fatima and Sara. We just wanted to tell you, you don't have to wear your *abaya* here."

"Thanks," I said, keeping it on to be contrary.

"So who's the *habarbish*?" Noor asked me.

"What?"

"That guy you came with."

"That's my uncle." Fatima and Sara tittered.

"No way!" Noor exclaimed. "But he's sooo Bedu!"

It took me a slow minute to get that she was using the word *Bedouin* the way an American might talk about rednecks. I replied thinly, "Is there something *wrong* with that?"

"It's just, he looks like the kind of guy who hangs around the mall staring at us 'cause he's unemployed with nothing better to do." Here Noor did an impression of a *habarbish*, with teeth bucked and eyes bulged.

"He's got a job," I retorted.

"I'm *sure* he does," Noor smirked.

My daily routine on school days started with the bathroom.

Despite the fact that the Gulf is the most water-stressed place on earth, for some reason the bathrooms *always* seemed to be sopping wet. In Umi's house there was no toilet paper. Instead we had a length of garden hose without a nozzle to wash with. The toilet was of the scary squat type, which meant I spent a lot of my time constipated with dread. The shower was a metal nozzle jutting out over the toilet and draining into a hole in the floor. Every morning I got up after *Fajer* prayer to take the first shower—if I waited too long into the morning the water tank on the roof turned into a boiling cauldron and left scald marks down my back.

In Falak's bedroom I'd change under my *jalabiya* so she couldn't see what I was wearing. I put on jeans and a T-shirt, and over them my school-uniform long skirt, so it appeared I was wearing my "proper" school clothes. Over that I wore my open *abaya* and *shala*. Lastly, when I left the house I'd toss the *shala* over my face to hide my identity from nosy neighbors. Riding with Faraj every morning and afternoon provided a neutralizing space, like going into the decontamination chamber before entering or exiting a space station. In addition to the neutrality of his presence, I was able to shed layers on the way to school in the following order:

First roundabout out of Madinat Al-Dafira—uncover face.

Inside school's front gate—*shala* off.

Locker—*abaya*.

Bathroom—skirt off.

Class—jeans and T-shirt.

When school let out I'd do the opposite. On the way home Faraj forced me to tell him all about the restricted *other* world I lived in. To Faraj it was *Lifestyles of the Rich and Famous*; to me, it was just confusing. He seemed endlessly curious about the rich kids and what their day-to-day lives were like. They were some of the very privileged few whom Faraj had only ever seen passing in Lambos along the corniche.

My situation had been thrown glaringly into focus by the proximity of my American and Arab worlds, which existed within a few roundabouts of each other. Despite the nearness, I managed to miss a lot of school at the beginning while Faraj and I got into a regular rhythm. Some mornings when he was late coming back from his night shift, I'd sit with Umi Safya in her room while she gave herself a shot of insulin and listened to the news on her little red Viking radio. She sat flat on the floor in a posture like a baby's: back straight, legs akimbo, coffee and dates and newspaper and Quran and radio and telephone arrayed around her like discarded toys.

She kept the cane alongside her at all times so that if the phone rang she could flip it off the hook and drag it toward her with its silver claw. I used the phone to call Faraj to wake him up, but he rarely answered. If the living room clock struck nine, well into first period, I'd just end up changing back into my *jalabiya* and going back to bed. When Faraj *did* get me to school I hopped out and raced into the hall, where I'd strip down to my jeans and Converse and toss my *abaya* in a wad into my locker. The commute between Madinat Al-Dafira and the American school began to give me cultural whiplash. I felt like a deep-sea diver, adjusting constantly to the pressures of the two very different environments. And just like the bends, it was painful.

It took stepping outside the tribal boundaries (something I hadn't ever done before) to see how Al-Dafira was perceived within the larger, national context. I discovered through being cornered in class discussions that apparently *we* were notorious for being backward, brutish barbarians who were culturally impenetrable even to fellow Qataris. According to my new classmates, Al-Dafira boys were "scary dudes"—backdunesmen and bumpkins who packed huge clubs called *ajeras* in their cars just in case of a skirmish. What was even more disconcerting to me was that no one seemed to know anything at all about the women I knew and loved.

Things should have started to get better as I began to figure out my place within the tribe, the school, and the city. I was now able to keep my *shala* on properly and had made friends with the Qatari girls at the school. The kids I was in school with were from power families, and I now started to understand that the relationship between my family and

theirs was analogous to that between the Wild and Won-
derful Whites of West Virginia and the Rockefellers. There
might be more of us, but numbers weren't everything.

I could see all sorts of things that wealth and the attendant cosmopolitanism that comes with prosperity and brisk
business travel had brought the Gulf. Equally, I was witness
to the fact that my family did not seem to be benefiting from
any of it. That said, we were by no means blameless for falling off the camel of "progress" in the night.

Generally speaking, my aunts, uncles, and even Flu were
mistrustful of the educational system. For this reason it was
common for kids in our family to miss large chunks of the
school year simply due to the widely held belief that long
desert camping trips were more valuable as education. In a
world where learning to scrape the meat from a lizard's back
was an important survival skill, Al-Dafira kids would have
thrived. However, that was not the world we were living in
anymore. As a rule, almost all of my cousins, both male and
female, were held back in school, and it was normal to drop
out to get married. The lack of success in school led to a generally negative collective opinion of it. This paved the way
for a generation of individuals who could survive alone in the
desert but who if placed at a desk were considered failures.
Needless to say, this general status of abjection was upset-
ting to me. In addition to this, my privileged place among
the wealthiest kids in the country only served to make me
feel more confused, more belligerent, and more alone than I
had ever been in America.

Umi Safya encouraged us not to care about being accepted by the "moderns," as the non-Bedouin city-folk were

referred to. Umi complained about how they had begun to impose ideas about class that had not existed before. "Nowadays, all the girls want weddings in fancy hotels, not tents, and they want personal drivers for shopping trips to spend money they don't have. They want *marka* handbags and shoes." And she was right—all of the Gulf had a bad case of the nouveaux riches. This was big trouble for other families like ours, because we had the nouveau part without the riche.

When I was just a visitor, no one expected me to pray. And when I was new, no one expected me to roust myself at 5 a.m. Now that I was a resident taking up my mouthful of the house's food rations, I was expected to pray *at least* three times a day. Umi entered in the dark every morning and jangled her cane through the rungs of the metal bunk bed like a dinner triangle, yelling "*Goomu! Al-Salah!*" It had come to pass by now that I was too ashamed to admit I didn't really have enough memorized to pray properly. I sat down on the bottom bunk and stared at Falak's back while she went about her prostrations. She looked like a ghost silhouetted in her soft white *khimar*, the only skin showing the soles of her feet, mottled orange from an old henna job. I listened to her prayers as I hunched there on the bed. She whispered a verse, words knocking against the backs of her teeth as she spoke them without opening her mouth. It was a soothing repetition. I imagined that holding those sounds in my mouth would be refreshing, like sucking on a mint.

When she left the room I locked the door behind her and timidly unrolled the carpet and *khimar* like a spiritual scavenger. I felt silly wrapped in my aunt's sheet, standing at the foot of her carpet, right hand over left at my belly. What could I do? I assured myself it would be the effort that counted, and I called the verses I could remember up from pit of my childhood memory. The first part came easily, and apart for a fumbled line in the middle, the full *Fatiha* tumbled out of me. But then I was at a loss, because the rest of the words were empty.

I gave up and knelt down on the carpet feeling like an idiot. My mind wandered the maze-line that bordered the carpet. It was bright electric blue, and for the first time I noticed that the design on the carpet was actually a view looking out through a colonnade to the *Kaaba*. I kept parsing through the verses I knew, tracing them with my finger in the Quran, wishing I understood, expecting some kind of epiphany to come from pronouncing the syllables. It reminded me of staring at a Magic Eye puzzle in the newspaper—retraining my vision into recognizing another dimension.

Then I had a moment of strange out-of-self objectivity, like the surprise when you look in the mirror and notice how alien and weird human faces really are. I felt shrinkingly small and epically distant from everyone and everything I knew. The earth was turning on its axis under me, and it was making me dizzy. That old star phobia started coming back and I wanted something to cling to. And as the situation would have it, that thing came in the form of a boy.

18

EPSILON CANIS MAJORIS •
THE VIRGINS • العذارى

Suhail and I were paired together during a physics unit on diffraction. It was unusual for Qataris of the opposite sex to be paired up, and in truth, the boys and girls generally kept a respectful distance from one another in school. There was a sort of silent but sacred Las Vegas bond between the Qataris—whatever happened in school stayed in school. Still, the girls were very careful about their appearance (perhaps no more so than image-obsessed teenage girls anywhere else), and the boys who loved kicking the backs of foreign girls' chairs adjusted their behavior when a Qatari girl was present. As these things generally go, I had noticed Suhail because he wasn't like the other boys. So when we finally sat beside each other, watching Mr. Kindi work out an equation on the whiteboard, I was sprung.

"The beam shape of a radar antenna can be analyzed using diffraction equations," Mr. Kindi explained in the background. The foreground of my brain was fizzing with the nearness of the boy next to me. "So today we are going to do a fun experiment with diffraction. Does anyone know

189

who this is?" He passed an envelope around the class with a thirty-five-dirham postage stamp on it.

"Ibn Haitham," Suhail said, too quietly to be heard.

I was impressed. His apparent fluency in Islamic science and his ability to recognize the smudgy little portrait were intimidating in themselves. But the thing that beguiled me most was his indifference to getting credit for it, a trait that was rare in a culture where practically every activity was given a résumé-padding certification and even the most minor milestone was commemorated with a trophy.

Someone at the front yelled out, "Ibn Haitham!"

"That is correct!" Mr. Kindi proclaimed, enthused by the response he was getting.

Suhail smiled in quiet triumph as though the praise had been lavished on him. And that was all it took. The little hairs on my body stood on end and reached for him. I was charged, lit, on. His presence was like a burning ember right next to me, and as I warmed myself in his aura, I also noticed things: his big white teeth as perfect as Chiclets, the mustache bristling his boyish face, the comet of depigmentation scarring his cheek . . . and I yearned, which was a new feeling.

"And what was he famous for having observed?" Mr. Kindi cut into my daydream. Shifty silence.

Again Suhail answered quietly, "Solar eclipse."

Mr. Kindi looked around the room hopefully. "Nobody?"

I nudged Suhail, exasperated for him. I grabbed his hand and raised it for him.

"Suhail, do you have the answer?" Mr. Kindi asked hopefully.

"He observed the eclipse of the sun."

"Extra credit to you, sir, good." Mr. Kindi turned his back to us and carried on with the lesson.

Suhail smiled at me, and I beamed back like a dope before sensing the gentle withdrawal of his hand from where I was still involuntarily gripping him. Rather than humiliate me (which I expected), Suhail carried on like normal, sharing the textbook and cooperating on the lab experiment, which was to build a functioning camera obscura.

The next Thursday, on the day of our unit quiz, he came to class with a note on folded-up graph paper. Suhail slipped it to me as he took his seat. Mr. Kindi handed out old Pee Chee folders as anti-cheat partitions, and my paramour disappeared behind the scribbled-over illustrations of young Americans playing basketball. Worried Mr. Kindi would think I was cheating, I managed to keep myself from opening the note in class. Suhail hadn't looked or even smiled at me like he usually did when he came into the room. I was certain it would contain either a cease-and-desist-looking-at-me-that-way order, or it would be a polite hint that maybe I ought to start using a different deodorant. By the time I escaped to a stall in the bathroom, my stomach was in such a nervous knot I was almost sick. I unfolded the note. I read what it said. I read it again. I panicked.

It said, in carefully practiced ballpoint, *I like you*.

The Gulf is an inhospitable place for young lovers. This much I knew from experience, tagging along with Faraj. The subterfuge involved gave even the most chaste relationship a contraband quality. But back then I had only been a kid—a mute, harmless, indifferent witness to my uncle's transgressions. Now, as I found myself falling in love for the first time under Faraj's watchful stewardship, I had some new thoughts about the way these things worked.

It must have taken tremendous courage for Suhail to write the note, and it was written with what I believed to be a certain effortless poetry. *"I like you,"* I repeated to myself. How could I resist? The weekend was a long and belabored process of drafting and redrafting a reply. What began as a fifteen-page panegyric I managed to whittle down to a trim five. Whatever unnamed urge had compelled me to run away from home was now driving me to run toward Suhail. Abstractly, I guess I understood that falling in love *here* might be the worst possible thing I could do. But when I lay awake and pined in my bunk bed, listening to my seven snoring aunts and cousins, I just didn't care.

Once we had established our status of reciprocated like, we were swept away and spent every break together. We kept a steady correspondence in carefully folded and sneakily exchanged notes. Although we were obviously interested in each other as bodies, there was a long period of telling that first went down. I say telling because it was similar to what therapy is meant to be like. I poured the entirety of me onto him in an eruption of memories and music and bile and half-baked ideas about what to do with my life, and in return was excited by his preferences and knowledge and ambitious plans for his promising future in planetary physics. We had a slew of unexpected things in common, including our love of *Al Amira Yakout*, dislike of Fonzies puff chips, and reverence for *Dune* and Carl Sagan. I gave him a mixtape of my favorite star-themed Bowie, Beck, and some appropriately angsty Fiona Apple. He burned me CDs of old Laiwa folk songs and taught me to how to strum his oud, which was the closest thing to a guitar in Doha.

Although we were intensely secretive, everybody knew. Suhail endured all kinds of harassment from the boys. "Qatari guys have dirty minds and big mouths, I'm just saying," Noor warned me. But Suhail obviously had neither of those things. He was the one who helped me navigate the dos and don'ts of the system. And I knew that the other Qatari kids respected Suhail for that, and therefore, whatever they might have thought about me, they wouldn't talk.

Whatever surplus energy I had after the transitioning from school to home and back was spent trying to outwit my uncle in order to slip away and see Suhail. Ironically, the double-bluff drop-off, the Family Day fake-out, and other Gulf classics of tactical creeping I had learned from Faraj himself. I put all of his inadvertent lessons to good use during the course of the year. And like his and Kholoud's ill-fated relationship, Suhail's and mine was clumsy and innocent and completely unequal to the spy levels of deception we employed to see each other.

When I had enrolled myself in the American school, Baba—who was still living in Abu Dhabi—swore Faraj and Falak to secrecy about the fact that my school was integrated. Although it was impossible to stop idle chat about the American girl, the one who danced, the one who fought with boys, the one who had crash-landed out of the sky and now expected acceptance, he still wanted to avoid as much gossip about me as he could. So as my male guardian in Doha, Faraj had an extra stake in ensuring that my honor remained intact. He had preemptively started to apply many of the same rules that had constrained his girlfriends, like Kholoud, to me. At least I knew where he got it from when he locked the door to the roof and took the key. This hypocrisy made me confrontational at the beginning and two-faced by the end. I let my anger at his hypocrisy simmer down and applied it instead to productive means of escape. However, Faraj had me checkmated for a while without even trying. The sheer volume of people in the house ensured that my phone calls were screened. I was only allowed to go to the mall with a chaperone. And Faraj cut into our after-school loitering by arriving on the dot every day and parking the humiliating *garumba* in a spot where he had a good vantage into the high school hallway.

Faraj did not do this because he suspected me of wrong-doing. But being sixteen and therefore equipped with an overblown sense of injustice, I was sure he was doing it on purpose. Now I understand that his reasons were twofold: The first, if misplaced, desire was to protect me from what appeared to him to be an unsafe environment. This concern was fair enough. Within our tribe, the awkwardness of my placeless situation was treated gently and sometimes (much to my annoyance) with pity. Comparatively little was expected of me, and as is often the case with those who have little to lose, they gave me everything—including the benefit of their doubt. But now I had entered into a hypercritical, ultrasensitive caste where the impartial rules of larger society would apply to me. If I were to misstep, however naive the fumble might be, the honor of my family would be at risk. The second of Faraj's reasons was less noble. With all this normalized socialization going on between boys and girls, Faraj was unable to keep his eyes in his head. I knew he meant well, but it was just embarrassing.

While the school days whizzed by in a fugue of touch-and-go contact with Suhail, my nights in our *beit shaabi* were gratingly slow. I mooched around the house, slumping from room to room and sighing. In the evenings I'd squeeze myself into a spot in the crammed *sala*, where I'd stare into the middle distance while my aunts and great-aunts reminisced about the old days. They exclaimed to Allah for forgiveness as they cackled at dirty jokes, which I was beginning to understand. Wool looped around their toes, my eldest aunts wove colored muzzles and straps to sell to moderns in the city who kept camels for show. But as I wafted around the house waiting for a chance to call Suhail, my mooning didn't escape *entirely* unnoticed.

Falak had inherited an old desktop PC from a university friend, and she now spent most of the day on the Internet trawling for pictures of exotic travel destinations and studio portraiture of fat babies. Her predilection for stockpiling screensavers didn't bother me in itself; in fact, I enjoyed watching her places-I'd-like-to-go slideshow. But with only one dial-up landline in the house, her Internet habit and my need for the phone rapidly escalated into a major point of contention between us. Desperate to call Suhail, there was more than one occasion when I snagged the phone cord under the door accidentally-on-purpose. I'd thread the cord as far as it would go, taking it off into a corner like a hungry animal. Often I'd hide out in the stairwell to the roof, where the winter blankets and mattresses offered some sound-proofing. Meanwhile, Suhail's and my epistles had reached fever pitch, and I had started to run out of places to hide them. The locked drawer in my desk was full and there was nowhere else that could guarantee safety from Falak's prying eyes or the hands of my younger cousins, who had free roam of the house while I was gone during the day. I bought a lockbox from the *dukkan* and Suhail kept his letters in the glove compartment of his Land Cruiser. We knew that one dropped note in the hallway could lead directly to our expulsion, public humiliation, and the wrath of his parents, my family, and both our tribes, in a worst-case scenario.

When we had run out of room for our letters, and with Falak's Internet appetite only growing, Suhail went out and bought me my first phone. It was a Nokia 3210. Sleek graphite cover with laser-green display. If ever there was a fetishized, beloved object, that phone was it. I kept it on silent so no one knew I had it, and whenever the little display strobed on and off, my heart flickered with excitement. At the time, it was still uncommon for girls in our family to have mobile phones. The excuse within our household had been that obviously the only thing a girl could possibly need a mobile for was to talk secretly to a boy. Although this was obviously true in my case, I still think the argument is ridiculous. After all, men were the ones who spent long hours calling random numbers until they struck gold with bored and anonymous girls willing to chat.

It was only a matter of time before Falak found out about my mobile and, for that matter, about Suhail. I came home one day to find a note on my bed. It read:

I know what you have been doing. You don't want to know what will happen if I tell anybody. These are my last words to you until you stop.

It took me a moment to register what her words meant and what exactly she was threatening me with. The note had been written aggressively, with the pen pressed hard onto the page and each letter beginning from the bottom rather than the top, the way Arabic natives write in foreign alphabets. It reminded me of the day Ma read my diary, Falak's tense penmanship making me flash back to Ma's clenched teeth. I felt guilty and betrayed at once. In response, I left a letter on her bed. It read simply, *It isn't what you think.* Falak climbed down the rungs of her bunk and, without reading it, wadded my note up and tossed it onto the floor before flicking the lights out on me.

After that, Falak continued to conspicuously ignore me. Now everyone in the house knew *something* was wrong, although I was grateful that at least Falak did not let on exactly what.

Suhail and I were both spooked after getting caught. We took a hiatus over the winter break, during which time we both made plans for the coming year. I was still pining, even though we had three classes together and lunches. He finished his college applications early and went to visit Cairo while I printed out an application to NYU and went camping with our family.

The whole house decided to go to a relative's camp somewhere north of Al-Hasa for the winter holiday. As we drove out toward the border, we passed the ever-expanding U.S. air base; the littlest kids packed themselves tight through the open sunroof so they could watch the F-16s and big cargo planes zoom overhead. Every time another jet boomed above us they whooped and ducked, and I thought briefly of Gramma's house and the sonic claps that used to rattle us back then.

When we got to camp, I staked a place in Uncle Mohamed's old Suburban where I could shelter from the wind, and filled a whole notebook with drafts of a personal essay for my application. In the evening I sat with Umi Safya and showed her the photos of smiling freshmen in the NYU prospective student pamphlet. We looked at a map of New York, and while we paged through the possibilities of a future, she asked me, "How many hours is it to drive to this place?" Considering her thorough knowledge of navigation by stars and ability to tell by the smell of the wind if clouds bore rain, her geographic innocence of where New York was came as a bit of a shock. But it shouldn't have been. Why would she ever need to know where the Big Apple was? Anything west of Jeddah was still of no interest to her.

The numbered forms asked a lot of questions I didn't know the answer to. For example, the space for permanent home address flummoxed me; I didn't know whether to apply as

a Qatari or an American, and the declaration-of-ethnicity
section was dispiriting. On official documentation throughout high school in Puyallup, I had always checked the box
for "Other," and when asked to "please specify," scribbled in
"Klingon." No one ever seemed to notice, and so it became
habit, the paperwork processed along with that of my peers
who had boxes to check for "Alaska Native," "Asian," "Asian-
American," "Native Hawaiian," "Samoan-American," and
"Other Pacific Islander." But this application was serious;
the selection of box might determine everything. I finished
the sentence "I identify" with "Other," and left the "please
specify" line blank.

Like it did for every "other" kid in the world raised on
American media, New York had always glowed distantly
in my mind as *the* place to go. I knew nothing about it,
knew no one there, and had no money to make it. But that
didn't matter; I still considered it the Mecca for me. When
questioned about my choice by Ma and Baba, I said they
just wouldn't understand. The city existed for me (and I
presume most other people who've never been there) as a
mashup of pop culture sedimented in layers by the decade,
a place where the streets were always wet and the lights
were extra bright. The city in my head was essentially a
cartoon. It had the cityscape of Gotham from *Batman:
The Animated Series*, everyone talked like the kids in *Kids*,
and, with the songs of *An American Tale* drilled deeply into
my head, I couldn't separate the Statue of Liberty from
a French pigeon in spats singing "Never Say Never." Even
though I knew my chances of getting into NYU were slim, I
filled out the application. When we returned to Doha from

the desert, I double-checked all the papers, slipped them into a manila envelope, kissed and sealed it, and gave it to Faraj to mail for me from the main post office and hoped for the best. Although we had drifted apart as I spent more time avoiding him than tagging along, Faraj was still my main link to the outside world.

After winter break, Suhail and I decided we had to see each other. I disguised it as a "feminine errand" in which I had to run to the Al-Rehab Ladies Saloon. The "saloon" was like a grown-up clubhouse and bore a large warning, "No Men Allowed." The windows were papered over with posters of relaxing European women. It always looked kind of threatening to me. Like a meth lab with a no-trespassing sign put up by some paranoid hillbillies. I disappeared behind the face of a smiling woman enjoying a mud mask, the cucumbers over her eyes making her look like a mantis. I waited for Faraj to drive off and then turned into the saloon. Somewhere beyond the entrance lobby there were multiple hair dryers blowing. The main room was designed like a *sala*, with cushions lining the walls and magazines like *Sayidaty* and *Snob al Hasna* stacked in the corners. A hefty Jordanian woman sat immobile in the middle of the room, her ankles propped up on tissue boxes while she waited for elaborate trails of fresh henna to dry. She watched me cross the room to where her baby was splashing around like a little bird in a Pedispa foot massager. I didn't look back at her as I slipped silently out the back door of the saloon and then up into Suhail's waiting Land Cruiser.

I hunkered down low, as flat as I could, and felt him pull

out onto the main road. "Hi!" I whispered from behind his seat. Suhail reached his hand back around the armrest for me to hold. His palms were sweaty. We drove across town to an empty compound Suhail had scouted. Ever since the early days of oil expatriation in the region, there have been compounds, and ever since there have been compounds they have been havens from the normal rules. In there, we'd be safe.

The New World Compound was full of empty, unlocked houses. They were rowed, all white angles of stucco and sunlight, waiting in anticipation for international oil employees to fill them up with their families. The small, picturesque streets were empty and had names like Bogota Boulevard and Austin Avenue. Some of the roads, like the houses, were still unfinished, smooth pavement cutting off into the rocky dust. Suhail parked his truck in a hidden area. We got out and passed together on foot through the ghost town, looking like skittish survivors of some rapture-style apocalypse, half expecting zombie security guards to leap out at any moment. Suhail led me to a villa at the far end of the compound. The front was covered in tatty tarp that blew in the wind like a shroud, and we stepped underneath it to peek in the front picture window. Even though it was brand new, the villa had the feeling of a ruin. It was the same spooky quality of a nuclear test house—still as a tomb, the pool empty, air clogged with suspense like a noxious fume.

Suhail and I sat together on the floor of the dining room. I asked him about his trip to Egypt over winter break: Had he gone to the pyramids? Seen any celebrities? Made it to the street where they made ouds? But he was bursting with some other news and was having a hard time keeping it down.

"What's up with you?" I asked.

"Guess!" he challenged me, bouncing up and down.

He reminded me of a little kid waiting for someone to open a present. It was infectious.

"Just tell me!"

"MIT!" he squealed.

I clapped and yelped my excitement for him. In a fit of joy he kissed me.

As it turned out, since Suhail had applied early he'd been given advance placement into the astrophysics course he had wanted. Better still, it was close to New York City. The sun angled through the window and across the empty space like a helicopter searchlight. And like the clock striking midnight, I was reminded that I didn't have long before I had to be back at the front door of the beauty "saloon," where Faraj would pick me up. "It's fate!" Suhail said over his shoulder as I slithered out and to the back door of the beauty parlor. "Now I just *know* you're going to get into NYU." I, however, was less certain.

After we'd established the corner house at the empty compound as our hideout, Suhail and I became bolder and snuck away to it more often. We minimized phone conversations and note-passing, as those things could be intercepted. I'd plant the seeds of an excuse with Faraj weeks in advance, and then Suhail and I would run through our plot briefly on the phone: pickup spots, drop-off locations, back roads to take. My relationship with Suhail replays in my mind more like a heist montage than the soft-focus meadow-frolic young love is supposed to be. The tension that led up to every carefully arranged meeting made every moment intense: the glimpse of one another from across a crowded intersection, a peck briefly stolen in the hall between classes, playing home in our empty house, pretending to swim in our empty pool.

As we approached the end of the year, we were getting lazy about covering our tracks. While Suhail made plans for his big move to America, I started to wonder if I'd ever even get my rejection letter from NYU. I might still be wondering about it today had I not dropped my Nokia down under the seat of Faraj's truck on the way back from school one day. I was rooting around blindly for the handset when I felt a familiar envelope deep under the seat. I didn't need to pull it out to know what it was, and I don't need to tell you that I thought it was the end of the world. Faraj had neglected to send my application.

I hurled myself into the backseat of the truck and blubbed, crying away my big New York dreams of a new career in a new town. But it wasn't the end of the world, not yet, anyway. Things had to get more discouraging first. After my initial meltdown, Ma and Baba each came back to me with plan Bs.

Baba called the house phone first with an idea: "My neighbor lady is very nice. She can teach you Quran lessons. Maybe you come here to Abu Dhabi, improve your Arabic!"

I hung up the phone. I would rather spelunk in a cave full of guano than spend time in that dismal Abu Dhabi government-housing block.

Ma's suggestion was no less bleak: "Well, you know, honey,

the military is not a bad option for you. In fact, it would do you some good. Teach you discipline, get you in shape. And if you *did* go to college, they'd pay for it!"

I remembered the type of person who used to go out for JROTC in school in America and shuddered at the thought of flag duty. I wouldn't last two seconds with that bunch of *World of Warcraft* and paintball veterans. After Ma hung up I hurled myself into a pillow and had a screaming fit that scared my little cousins into hiding.

That night I went onto the roof to call Suhail. He pieced together the story through my sobs. I lay on my back watching a little red satellite cross the night, blinking through my tears. He promised he'd come up with another plan B for me too, and said I should arrange to meet him after school the next day. He only had a few weeks before leaving. His father was so proud of the MIT acceptance that he had offered to buy Suhail an apartment and set up a home for him in the States. Knowing this might be our last meeting made things urgent. But the slew of bad news wasn't over yet. The next day the principal called me into his office and informed me that without payment of tuition within the next two weeks, I wouldn't receive my diploma.

That afternoon, Suhail picked me up from a bank of bushes near the beach at the Sheraton. As usual, I lay down flat in the back and we played a game where I guessed our location based on things viewable from my angle. I called them while he drove: "Rainbow!" "Oryx!" "Crazy Signal!" When we got to our secret house I collapsed in his arms, waiting to hear his plan B, hoping it would save me. He knew a guy who knew someone who could get me into a university without my having to apply. There was no deadline—I just had to gather some papers from school, write a letter, and give it all to Suhail.

"You could just go there for a little while so you don't fall behind, and then transfer to NYU once you get accepted next semester."

"If," I corrected him. But I already felt better. Just a half hour with Suhail seemed to tap so deeply into my oxytocin levels that I didn't even care where it was I'd be going. "So where is it?" I asked as an afterthought from the back of his car as we drove back.

"Cairo."

"Cairo," I repeated to myself. I had no cartoon image of Cairo in my head, unlike New York, but I did have the Egyptian accents of every Arabic-dubbed Disney film to go by. I was just wondering how one would translate the song "There Are No Cats in America" when Suhail slammed on the brakes and I tumbled up over the seat.

"Shit," he said, glancing into his rearview mirror. I didn't need to turn my head to know.

We'd been caught. Faraj was early, parked by the main entrance of the hotel. It wasn't exactly in flagrante, but to Faraj the circumstantial evidence was enough. "I'm so sorry!" I whispered to Suhail, and scrambled out.

Faraj put me, cop-style, into the backseat and slammed the door, catching my *abaya* with it. He walked around the front of the car and glared back through the headlights at Suhail, scanning his license plate and dialing my father at once. I willed Baba to pick up the phone; he would be able to explain a way out for me. But he wasn't answering his phone. I was on my own.

"It's not what you think!" I shouted at Faraj as we drove off and I wept in the backseat. Kohl striped my cheeks like claw marks and I swallowed back my whimpers while frantically texting Suhail.

"Did you think your uncle is an idiot?"

Faraj wrestled my Nokia out of my hands and threw it out the window. I howled and spun in my seat to look out the back windshield. I saw my little green light forlorn in the darkness of the street. It flashed on and off for a moment—I was sure it was Suhail calling—but then it disappeared under the treads of a big sweet-water truck.

Faraj took his place beside Falak in the silent treatment for the remainder of the semester, while Suhail and I skulked in the hall after school, looking longingly at each other out of Faraj's sight. That month was spent in a sort of mourning period for our imminent separation. As much as it was a time of sorrow over having to part, there were a few miraculous events that made it easier to cope. For one, with Suhail's help I was accepted into the American University in Cairo. No boot camp or Quran lessons after all. I was to start immediately during the summer semester to catch up on my modern standard Arabic. And second—what of the financial hurdles of tuition in Doha and international student rates in Cairo? In short, through the help of certain advocates in the school, my situation caught the attention of a powerful but secret patron who takes education very seriously. A proxy (imagine Mr. Pumblechook in an *abaya*) was sent to Umi Safya's house to confirm the direness of my straits. A week before graduation, I was extracted like Pip Pirrip from my home and given the message that *some-one* had great expectations for me. Qatar is in many ways a place where miracles happen, and to that individual, who personally saw to it that I would receive an education—I will *always* be grateful.

19

DELTA VIRGINIS •
THE HOWLER • العوّاء

If I felt like Pip being rescued from my lot in Doha, arriving in Cairo made me feel like Luke Skywalker entering into Mos Eisley—fresh off the moisture farm. The time between being plucked from my lowly lot in Doha and landing in Egypt had only been a matter of weeks, so my head was spinning. A gruff man eyed me as I came out into the parking lot of the airport. He was leaning against a flamboyantly decorated cab decaled with hearts and cartoon blood drips as though it had just hit and run. "Going somewhere?" he grunted at me through a puff of Cleopatra cigarette. I peered around for other options, but strangely, no one else was vulturing for my fare. I got into the car and was whisked across town via the Sixth of October Bridge.

The ride was improbably smooth as we hurtled through the tangled lanes, and even though he was steering with only one finger, the driver guided us as surely as if we were on a maglev track. We sped above the old Cairo, squeezing at high speed between minibuses and motorcycles like a Fiat hovercraft. Neon-lined minarets and fluorescent-lit office blocks whizzed by in my periphery, and I dug my fingers into the ripped foam of the backseat for dear life. It looked oddly futuristic for such an ancient city. But first impressions fade, and anything probably would have dazzled me coming from the gravelly backwater that Doha still was at the turn of the millennium. I rolled down my window as we crossed over the Nile. It was dotted with little colored lights, pleasure boats blasting festive party music from busted speakers as they passed under us in the snaking black current.

At seventeen, I'd never been to a real metropolis before. Tacoma, Seattle, Abu Dhabi, Doha—although they were technically cities, they were all quaint hamlets in comparison to this. Equal parts disoriented and exhilarated, I wondered what Suhail might be doing at that exact moment all the way in Boston and felt all the frustration and fears of the past months burn off as we descended into my new home.

The first order of the next day was to go to the Qatari Ladies Home, where I could stay for free. It was on a leafy street in Mohandeseen, innocuous from the outside, wretched on the inside. The officious proprietor gave me the full tour. Although she was Egyptian, she had carefully studied the details of being a fine Qatari lady, and so, similar to religious converts, she felt the need to compensate by out-Qatari-ing Qataris. She wore a *very* sleek age-inappropriate *abaya* and lots of ostentatious jewelry. She carried a very expensive Louis Vuitton wallet, gesticulating with it while she gave me her tour of the building. She listed their facilities: satellite television, a fleet of drivers, and so on. Every tenant had two maids to look after her—one to clean and one to cook. As ludicrously decadent as all this sounds, the rooms were all deeply dismal. As we made our way through the halls, she opened different apartment doors at random without knocking, surprising the wan-looking girls behind them. Disinfectant evaporated off damp cement floors as she bragged, "The maids are all live-in." She led me to a scene of maids who were old enough to be the students' grandmothers having lunch and watching TV in a little staff room.

When we returned to her office, she seemed confident that her tour had sufficiently impressed me and took out a stack of papers for me to sign while she rattled off the rules like fine print.

"The curfew is five p.m. every night but for Thursdays, when you are allowed to go to a restaurant for dinner."

I almost choked. Even if this place was free of charge, I couldn't move backward on the track I'd laid away from the constraints of Puyallup and Doha. I needed a place where Suhail could come and stay. I gave my excuse: "I'm unsure how this would work. You see, I have class until eight p.m. on some nights."

She barely restrained a sneer as she eyed me up and down; to her that sounded like a *fine* excuse for getting up to no good. I would have done anything to dodge falling under this lady's matron law. "Well, *habibti*, perhaps this is *not* the home for you after all."

The university's hostel was my next option, and I was disappointed to find that it was full of Americans and Gulf Arabs. Because the dorm was full of CIA wannabes and daughters of sheikhs, I kept to myself, knowing we'd have nothing in common to talk about. I spent my first week trying unsuccessfully to get through on the phone to Suhail and the next sulking in the computer lab. I felt trapped by my jealousy and wrote mortifying, bitter e-mails to Suhail as a way of distracting myself from the stray place I now found myself stranded in.

The American University in Cairo was the kind of place everyone in Egypt had heard of but knew nothing about. I knew nothing about it at all when I arrived, but soon found that it was elite and mysterious in the same way the American school in Doha had seemed to Faraj. And just like in Doha, I found myself having to make tiresome explanations about where I was coming from to the people I was categorized with. The demographic of AUC was split up into generalized ranks, the cracks of which I slipped through. The vast majority of the university was composed of advantaged Egyptians pursuing full four-year degrees in computer science or broadcast journalism. The next largest group was foreign exchange students on study-abroad programs. Among them were cliques of hippies from Evergreen in Washington State, poli-sci majors from Georgetown, and Muslim-American kids from all over just wanting to study Arabic. Those were the main draws for the U.S. intake. The rest of the students were wonderfully assorted: sons of Palestinian politicians, Japanese Egyptology *otaku*, Swedish human rights researchers, exiled African intellectuals, and a disproportionately large number of Bohra women from India who were nicknamed "Bo-Peeps" on campus for their frilly Muslim dress.

In 2001, the American University in Cairo still consisted of three main campuses huddled together at the southeastern lip of Tahrir Square. The most iconic of these was "Main." It was a gorgeous stone building constructed in the 1860s for the Minister of Education, Khairy Pasha. Ornery cats roamed the maze of tiny halls, and from the roof I could stand and watch the five-story palm trees sway peacefully in the exhaust fumes wafting up from Tahrir Square. The second campus, "Greek," was a Brutalist cement fortress consisting of the sociology and journalism departments, as well as the library. On entry there were huge double-wide steps forming the main promenade. It had a reputation as a catwalk, which everyone entering the campus was subjected to, and a meeting place, which meant there was always a big audience when you walked by. Farther afield there was "Falaki" and "Rare"—the first named after the nineteenth-century Egyptian astronomer, the second after the type of books it housed. Falaki was a modern building housing the art and computer departments, and Rare was the kind of library/lecture hall in which you could imagine Aleister Crowley fingering through the card catalogue for "Pharaonic curse."

The walk to these outlying campuses was infamous, as schoolboys from the nearby Lycée came to ogle, grab, and generally harass the women who were bitterly assumed by the neighborhood to be the spoiled daughters of Egypt's most powerful and wealthy. Some of these kids were no more than ten, and they really didn't care who you were. As long as you had tits, they were looking for an in. And by *in*, I mean the passing chance to grab a handful of private flesh and groan grotesquely at you.

I spent the first week on campus pinging from office to office and eating for free at new-student orientations. My assumption that entering the fold as a Qatari would simplify things was a mistake. Rather than allowing me to disappear into the flock with my Arab peers as I'd hoped, it had two adverse effects. First, the university assumed that as a Gulf Arab I was wealthy and therefore ineligible for any kind of scholarship or work-study situation. Second, I was forced to sit for remedial English aptitude tests and was automatically enrolled in college-level Arabic. The first day of class we were required to write our opinions on a very complicated article about pan-Arabism, which the class had deconstructed together while I was sitting with them. I struggled to follow as the professor, a jowly man called Dr. Zaydan, rattled on about the essay and then opened the floor for discussion. I took down the best notes I could, finally piecing them with my dictionary's help into a single unreadable sentence I inferred to mean something like "The Arab personal identification she has no borders."

After class I approached Dr. Zaydan to plead my case. There was no way I would be able to endure an entire semester being beaten with my own linguistic weaknesses. But Dr. Zaydan was suspicious from decades of lazy students trying to avoid hard work. He managed to twist my qualms in my mouth and make me feel like a dunce in a few sharp words. He leaned back in his chair and looked over the frames of his glasses at the enrollment list. He ran his finger down it, found me, tapped my name, laced his fingers, and looked up at me with a fake-patient smile.

"Explain to me, Miss Al-Dafira, why do you need to be in a different class?"

"Because my Arabic is broken."

"This class is here to fix it. All of your peers have broken Arabic. What makes you think you are a special case?"

He said this with a mocking upswing in his voice, as though he had never heard of something so absurd. The only way out was to authenticate my inauthenticity. I began a monologue in Gulf pidgin about my origins, hoping that the combination of bad grammar, bad accent, and misused vocabulary would convince him. But it only seemed to make him angry.

"Don't try that stuttering Arabic with me. I lived in the Gulf. I know your family. You are the original Arabs! The nomads of the nomads! The Arabic language originates with your people! You should be proud."

I felt my face getting hot. This blow was low. "I *am* proud," I retorted, a little confused over how he knew who my family was and to hear that the language I learned in Umi Safya's house might be more than a dying dialect.

Dr. Zaydan continued, "You are more proud of your American culture, aren't you? You *must* be. You give English precedence over Arabic because it is easy."

"Doesn't everyone speak their mother tongue first?" I stuck up for myself.

"Believe me, you are not the first to beg exemption from my course. Your generation is lazy!"

The more he ranted, the more he seemed to convince himself that I was trying to con him. I didn't even need to speak. Apparently I had touched a nerve.

"Yes. You want to migrate into English! A primitive language! And you want to forget your noble origins."

I took the moment of silence to slip something in edgewise. "I don't know how I can prove it to you, doctor."

He sighed, unenrolling me from the class by crossing my name off his list. "Well, Miss Al-Dafira, you can't."

Two days later, just halfway through the first week, I had settled all my courses except for a replacement for Arabic. I finally tested into a modern Arabic literature in translation class instead, where the reading list included *Season of Migration to the North* by Tayeb Salih, *Adrift on the Nile* by Naguib Mahfouz, and *Zaat* by Sonallah Ibrahim. From the back of the class on the top floor of the main campus I had a good view of the square and the traffic below. Conversation at AUC was *always* political, despite the relative class-homogeneity of the students who attended. In this particular course, I had learned early on to stay out of it, as Mohamed, the wispy-bearded son of a prominent Muslim Brotherhood figure, and Magda, the outspoken daughter of a university professor, argued over whether Nawal El Saadawi was a shit-stirrer or a saint. We had just watched a documentary about the notorious Egyptian feminist Nawal El Saadawi to augment our reading of *Woman at Point Zero*, which had thrown the class into three consecutive days of maddening circular debate. I had received tacit hints during the summer semester that certain subjects were best left for Egyptians to debate. This was one of them. Still, although the class was full of born-and-bred Egyptians, it was Magda and Mohamed who dominated the class discussions while the professor looked on with mild amusement. These two contrary young Egyptians were so fully and impressively themselves that when they spoke, no one questioned them, not even the professor. The words they used, the clothes they wore, the little signifiers like Mohamed's baby *zebiba* prayer mark and Magda's pierced nose, were all consistent with who they were. I knew one needed a strong foundation from which to argue so persuasively, and equally I knew that I shouldn't wallow over the fact that I had no base to argue from. I envied Magda's eloquence. And however often Mohamed said things that made me want to weed-whack his beard, I *did* admire his passion.

On one of these afternoons, Mohamed and Magda were talking over each other when I noticed a large pink grasshopper staring up at me from the windowsill. Its segmented armor was a shocking color of pure-process magenta. For eyes it had smooth pea-size bumps. Like a marooned alien dragging itself across a lunar landscape, it made it halfway across the dusty ledge before I recognized it was injured, the back of it splayed out and broken as if it had only barely escaped someone's footfall. I looked down into the garden below, where a groundskeeper was tromping along using his leaf blower to clear a path through the leaves. Only these leaves were also candy pink. Then I recognized that he was blowing dead locusts around as they collapsed into the grass from the sky. Thousands of them, poisoned from gorging on pesticide-doused plants on farms outside the city. Then the rest of the class noticed the sky over Tahrir darken briefly as if by smoke. I gasped. The air was full—millions of flitting fuchsia streaks. Everyone came to the window to see. Despite the blind hordes smacking against the window, Mohamed and Magda persisted in their argument. It was the first locust assault on the city in this generation's memory, *just* momentous enough for us to be dismissed from class.

I walked backward into the swarm as I crossed Tahrir in the direction of home. There wasn't a single cab, and drivers were wiping pink mash from their windshields. I came to Qasr el Nil Bridge, where I saw a man standing in the mottled light, watching me. Unlike the distant figures I saw running for cover near the Mogama and on the other side of the bridge, he seemed unbothered by the plague of locusts that roiled overhead, avoiding the river. This was only my fourth month in Cairo, and the anger I was feeling toward men had worked up a good head of steam.

During the coming five years in Egypt, I would be catcalled, dirty-talked, insulted, felt up, slapped, hotly breathed upon, and groped. There would be confrontations—*many* of them. There would be cabbies who jerked off in front of me, there would be a soccer mob who dragged me out of a car to mass grope me, and there would be countless other scary and dangerous situations. Worst of all, I would be blamed for all of them. Scolded by onlookers, police, and even my father: "Well, maybe you shouldn't have been there, wearing that, at this hour." As a result of the regular bouts of molestation, I went through waves of retaliation, trying out various tactics to have my revenge. Mace worked well for me after I figured out Rule 1: don't spray *into* the wind. There were many hours spent in police stations pleading my case, many meetings with women's rights NGOs. And yet I never did learn how to deal with this particular aspect of living in Cairo. I suspect that few women have.

But back to the bridge. I was almost to the middle of the walkway when he postured himself defensively to prevent my crossing. Apparently he had a toll to collect before allowing me to pass. That toll was, of course, a riddle. A riddle I definitely didn't have the answer to.

"Where from?" he barked as I drew near. In his mouth "Wherefrum?" didn't seem like words at all. To me it sounded rude, this guy's bad idea of a mating call. I wondered if he might be crazy. Who would be out here in the open in the middle of this swarm of insects? Emboldened by the emptiness of the road, he stepped into my path and croaked out another charming disyllabic come-on: "Howmuch?"

I skittered off to the side trying to circumnavigate this self-appointed bridge-keeper, but I didn't move fast enough. Then I saw what it was he wanted me to look at. Shock like rigor mortis worked its way out of my body from the toes up. His *thing* stuck out brightly against the open fly of his slacks. It branded itself upon my brain like some kind of sick joke while it jutted there in the open, the same horrible, raw pink color as the locusts. He thrust it at me.

Bile rose up in my throat at the sight of his flappy thing, and I wished I could projectile vomit on command. A surge of adrenaline went gushing into my right arm. It shot out like it was possessed and pushed his chest out of my way at the very same moment he let out a spittle-ridden kissy noise. What happened next was in slow motion. His skin flushed a ruddy tone of red. I'd see the switch many times in the years to come. What starts as just having a bit of fun teasing a girl alters into an excuse to do her harm. His eyes widened and his cheeks shuddered with anger and then *thunk*! I heard nothing. He had punched me in the head. Suddenly lying flat on the road, I saw the treads of a tire narrowly miss me. I rolled over to right myself and saw the Fiat screech to a stop. I got up from the street, shaking with rage more than pain. The length of my skirt was soaking wet and clinging from the gutter full of candy-colored pieces of bug. The driver came running back to me. She led me away from the scene and drove me to a police station on the island. My assailant let out a mighty cuss as we drove off, but I won't repeat it. As we drove I saw a policeman taking shelter from the bugs under the paws of the great lions guarding the bridge.

At the entrance of the police station I was greeted by a young policeman smoking a cigarette with his rifle across his knees; his face glowed when he dragged the light off his smoke.

"I want to report someone for harassment," I said.

"Not my jurisdiction." He shrugged.

The lady driver clicked her tongue at him. "Shame on you. This girl needs help."

"Who touched who first?" the cop asked, bored.

"I did."

"So why are you complaining?"

"Because he . . . exposed himself to me and was saying rude words."

"What do you want us to do about something you can't prove?"

"He threw me into the street! He punched me in the head!"

The woman driver chimed in, "He did punch her, and I almost hit her."

"What can we do? She initiated it by touching him first."

"I did *not* hit him. I pushed him away from me."

"It's still touching, and so you are to blame." Blank face. Silence.

"Can I see who's in charge here?" I asked, fuming.

The lady driver advised I give up and go home. She offered me a ride, but I refused. This would only be the first of what ended up being many futile attempts at legal recourse, and like all those that followed, my words were twisted in my mouth and I went from victim to suspect.

The policeman led me into the station. "ID?"

I passed him a passport.

The young cop flipped through forward and back before I realized my mistake. "There is no visa to Egypt here. Where's your visa?" My conviction dropped out from under me. "Come with me," he said sternly.

I followed him into a little tiled room with high windows where a man in an epauletted black sweater sat, legs apart, on a rolling office chair. The day's newspapers were spread over a table; a sticky cup of Lipton bled an orange ring into a full-page spread of Mubarak in sunglasses. A small television with a satellite box sat on one corner of the table and beside this lay a black handgun. A standard-issue Beretta, so completely matte black it looked like a spray-painted toy.

"What's the problem?" he asked the officer who was dealing with me.

"She's got no visa."

"Wait! You're missing the point! I want to report someone for physical assault!"

"What nationality?" the commander spoke through me.

"I gave *him* my passport." I pointed at the young cop who

flung my blue passport out of my reach to the commander as if they were playing keep-away.

The commander thumbed through it with one hand. He shut the passport and had a long look at the TV, where the comedian Zakia Zakaria was in a downtown street wearing drag. He was performing for stunned members of the public.

The chief addressed me without looking away from the spectacle. "Miss, can you tell me what you're here for again?"

I could tell he was annoyed at this interruption of his program. I had a hard time modulating my voice now. "I want to report a man who harass—" I stopped to look at the young cop who was trying to hold back a laugh, cheeks bullfrogging. Was he laughing at the outraged newspaper salesman who was fighting Zakiah Zakaria off, or at my apparently ridiculous request for help? Tears of frustration were close. A commercial for Close-Up toothpaste came on, and they returned their attention to me.

"Why are you here in Egypt?"

Good question, I thought to myself and gave him the abridged answer, "I'm studying."

"And I see your last name is Al-Dafira. What are you really?" the cop asked. I bristled at the question and pretended not to understand. "*What* are you?" was only the slightest variation on my attacker's jibe "Wherefrum?" And I knew he was really only asking which part of the Arab world I was from.

His lackey called out a few guesses. "Jordanian? Moroccan?" This was classic.

When I refused to fess up he decided to play rough.

"Well, we can't let you go, miss, if you can't explain your lack of a visa."

The commander told the younger one to leave. And what he said next wasn't spoken with tenderness, it was a threat. "All you have to do is explain to me who you are. Your passport tells me foreign, which means you can't be here without a visa. But your name tells me something else. So just *say* it. *Anti Arabiya wella egnabia?*" Are you an Arab or a foreigner?

In this situation I knew which answer might appeal to his better nature. "*Ana Arabia*," I croaked like some inspirational chorus to a pop song, "I'm an Arab woman." For the first time the "ain" hooking out of the word declared it was true. And then, as if all I'd had to do was admit it, he flicked my passport across the desk. "That wasn't so hard, was it? Now go," he said, and waved me off. I left the police station feeling confused. What was going on!? How had the situation turned out like this? Why wasn't Suhail returning my calls or e-mails? Where was I going to go from here?

A week later, once the locusts had been swept up by the street sweepers and I'd simmered down from my encounter with the police, I emerged from the lit-in-translation class one afternoon and noticed a crowd gathering around a security guard's television set outside the campus. I crossed Mohamed Mahmoud Street with my head in another Nawal El Saadawi book. I passed a *shisha* café where another TV was blasting, surrounded by onlookers. It was a tiny place, mirrors covering its walls with a television as its centerpiece. With all the grave people gathering around, it reminded me of a shrine.

It was there that I saw the second plane hit. A unified yelp went up from the crowd as it happened, followed by questions about whether it was live or not. The proprietor of the café turned the volume up. I could hear the American anchor's voice, unnervingly shrill through the live Arabic translation. I registered gray smoke billowing out of a tower but didn't guess where in the world it might be. The only thing I had to compare it to was distant memories of the Oklahoma City bombing on the evening news at Gramma's house. I heard the anchor on TV say "New York City." My first reaction was one of surprise, *That's New York?* We all gasped together as the silhouette of a human launched itself out a window. A body falling from the sky lent terrible perspective to the dimension of the disaster, and was an access point to understanding the scale of what was happening.

That night I watched in the lounge on the female side of the dormitory. All the Gulfie and American foreign students were sprawled out with popcorn and candy. They had gathered to watch *Friends* but ended up snagged on CNN, where the constant refrain was "It feels like a movie." We sat in our *jalabiya*s and pajamas watching the reports: eyewitness accounts from the dust-covered people on the streets, wildly variant death toll estimates, and half-cocked theories about who could be responsible for this. Everything from kamikaze revenge for Hiroshima and Nagasaki to a Charles Manson killer-cult. These were all so cockeyed in hindsight.

"Please don't let it be an Arab." One of the Kuwaiti girls

voiced what many of us were thinking. No words I write could even begin to touch the horror of the event, but whether in New York or Cairo, *everyone* was afraid.

By the end of that week, we had all started to get repetitive stress headaches from the TV. The frantic loops of conversation and the patter of car commercial/horrific images/insurance ads were the symbolic externalization of all our internal monologues, wavering back and forth between empathy and self-involvement. The rest of the semester was spent in a sort of limbo. Crippled by the exodus of international students, some of my classes were canceled or postponed. I still waited for Suhail's e-mails. He only occasionally wrote to me, which I guess meant Boston was treating him well. When he did write to me, it was with vague suggestions of how and when he might come to visit Cairo. I measured how much he cared by how many kilobytes his e-mails were. Most often he mentioned wanting to visit so we could "be alone together," which was his euphemism for the eventual consummation of our relationship. Then he'd recede from contact for weeks while I camped in the dormitory computer lab faithfully refreshing my Hotmail, deleting spam, and searching Yahoo! for my last name, which mostly yielded images of mullet-sporting terror suspects and race-car drivers. The mug shots of rumpled Al-Dafira men always led me back to conspiracy theory pages and national security websites, a whirlpool down which I would sometimes get lost late into the night, a real-life cyber replacement for the paranoid dystopian narratives I used to love reading.

After the attacks on New York, a jagged tension pinched

the campus. All the entrances to and from the university were reinforced with metal detectors and armed police. The dormitory emptied of many American students, recalled by their universities or parents or scared off on their own. By this time I was sick of being insulated in the dormitory; I was also running out of money from my scholarship to pay for it. I knew a home of my own with no maids or roommates or television would be a tiny fraction of the price, and if I managed to find an apartment, Suhail could come to visit without any problems. I started my search going door-to-door downtown. Usually these buildings had begun life in Cairo's belle Epoque and had a disintegrated elegance that made my imagination run wild. Many of these buildings were rent-controlled, and so some entire buildings remained vacant, the owners preferring to leave them empty rather than deal with the hassle of tenants. Most landlords I met were doctors, lawyers, or retired police officials who regimented their lives around oily Turkish coffee, cigarettes, and thirty-year-old paperwork they kept shuffling around in the dining room sideboard.

When my pavement-pounding didn't turn up a home, I finally caved and allowed a very pushy *simsar* named Ahmed to assist me. He promised he'd find me something "sooberdalucks," by which he meant "super deluxe," by which he meant it had hot water and wasn't a bug colony. Many of the flats were both charming and foreboding, as was Ahmed, for that matter. He looked commandingly into my eyes as if he were trying to use the Force: "You *will* love this one." Before entering each apartment he would pause to say, "For real, miss, this apartment." He pinched his fingers before his lips and kissed them into a blossom—"Sooberdalucks!"

We had come to the end of a long day's search, and setting my purse down on a sideboard in a hallway, I let Ahmed show me around yet another place.

"Satellite! Washing machina! Balcona!"

He took me into the inner chambers of the apartment and opened the bedroom window to reveal an inaccessible dead space looking into the windows of the adjacent block. Fallen laundry and soda cans littered the ground below, and above were ten stories with a hexagon of sky barely visible beyond the protuberant butts of air conditioners. The rest of the flat was furnished in a pan-cultural retro-maniacal mishmash: a golden Louis XIV couch squatted defiantly in the middle of a spare living-room set. Zebra-skin carpets lined the room wall to wall, a clock in the shape of the mosque at Medina rang the hour, and the walls were covered with ugly papyrus souvenirs and bucolic paintings of the English countryside. This apartment was more confused about its identity than I was.

"I'm sorry, it's super, but just a little too deluxe," I said, turning to address Ahmed.

But the room was empty, silent but for a dusty wind blowing in through the fly screen and ruffling the potpourri flowers. I rushed to the sideboard where I had left my purse—gone! I imagined the passport inside the secret compartment of my bag. Everything that was officially me on paper had vanished. It had happened in a flash, just like that. I skidded down the stairs of the apartment building and out into the busy street, where I paced from one end to the other half-shouting to no one, "Help!" After my previous trouble at the police station, I knew I'd get no sympathy there. Ahmed was long gone and, for all official purposes, so was I.

I reported the theft to the embassy but they just advised me to wait a few weeks before undergoing the whole process. Maybe someone would turn my purse in, they assured me. I doubted it. With my rental possibilities severely impaired by the fact I had no valid identification, I reconcentrated my search on under-the-table sublets. After many shady dealings, I finally found a landlady who would exempt me from the tenant registration required by law if I paid a premium rate and kept to myself. It was a precarious situation in more ways than one. The landlord could ask me to leave without notice, and it so happened that the room she had to offer me was on a houseboat. She led me across the river from her chintzy Zamalek flat to her properties off Kit Kat Square, then farther down to Imbaba. This is where the banks of the Nile were moored with decrepit pastel houseboats full of ready-to-let, no-questions-asked, cheap rooms available for junkies, expats, and all type of wayward strays and suspicious persons who I guessed were now my people.

I wrote an e-mail to Suhail letting him know I was moving. He hadn't written in at least a month, and I veered between pining for and hating him. While he was absent from my regular days, he was still a real presence as important as Ma or Baba. After all, Suhail had helped to shape the way I saw myself and my future. Still, the only thing that made his silence bearable was the idea of nesting down on my own in a new life where no one knew me or would bother me about where I was from. I could reinvent myself in a room of my own, begin from a blank page, like enjoying the moments before writing in a fresh notebook full of virgin paper. I moved into the tiny space and made myself my first home, which floated in a river running through a city that, for all its frustration, brought me the closest I'd yet felt to being free as it sprawled between whatever East was and wherever West began.

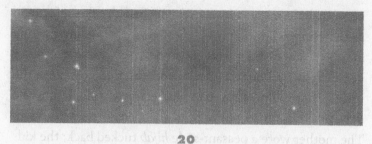

20

ETA CANIS MAJORIS •
THE MAIDENHEAD • العذره

Seedy would have been a compliment to describe my new houseboat home. When the river was low, the pilings anchoring it into the silt looked like the spindly legs of a man who'd been depantsed. It was more like a paddle-less double-decker Mississippi steamboat than an idyllic Norfolk fen barge. Toilet-blue paint warped along the mildewed waterline, and it was so full of holes it would sink if anyone were ever dumb enough to try to float it. When I arrived at my new home, the combination gardener and *bowab*, Hanafi, bounded up the stairs to meet me. He relieved me of my baggage while I haggled pointlessly (an unflattering habit for a foreigner) with the cabdriver in the street. By the time I'd gypped the driver out of about fifteen cents, Hanafi was already across the gangplank and depositing the suitcase in my little room. That night I lay awake, freaked out by distant wails coming from somewhere farther upstream than I'd ever ventured. The scuttle of river rats under the floor planks and the creaking of the wood between me and the water eventually dipped and swayed me to sleep.

The next morning I awoke at sunrise to a loud thumping

noise outside my window. I rose to find the face of a man at the window staring in at me. He was standing floating in a boat, knocking a stubby wooden oar against the outer helm of my bedroom. His wife and children nestled in the little skiff, pulling in a web of blue-green netting. I drew the dust-caked curtains but kept a slit open to peek through. The mother wore a peasant-style *hijab* tucked back; the kids were small and bedraggled enough to be of unidentifiable sex. Their tools, pans, and laundry were arrayed around the tiny, self-contained vessel. As they bobbed away down the side of the boat, still knocking to scare the fish out from underneath, I could see the name of their boat in bright yellow paint: "Sunny." The boat started to lurch, dragged to the side by the net, which was caught somewhere underneath the stilts of the houseboat. The woman was fast and she flashed a paring knife out. She began cutting parts of the net away and letting it sink back into the river. In moments they were free again, the whole family back adrift together. I thought of Ma and Baba and Dima, all of us cast to far-off parts of the world, and wondered if we'd ever be in the same boat together.

I'm not sure it's possible to be truly alone in a city like Cairo. Although I felt alone, between the rats under the floorboards, the fishing families on the river, and my upstairs neighbors, I definitely wasn't. The upstairs apartment was a scene straight out of the houseboat in the Mahfouz book (and famous Adel Adham film) we'd read in class the semester before, *Adrift on the Nile*. The second-story apartment was host to a revolving set of young Egyptian men in various stages of religious devotion and hedonistic rebellion. They were journalists, law students, Sufis, and junkies, and many of them went by nicknames like Freetz, BonBon, and Turbo. I lay awake listening to their chitchat most nights with my balcony door open. They were smart but pompous, clouded with hash, quoting Sayyid Qutb and Michel Foucault in the same breath. They listened alternately to Adaweya and Pink Floyd, and although their musical taste irked me, their voices were a comfort on nights when the horrible wailing echoed down from upstream.

Resentment of Suhail's silence was threatening to grow over me like a dark mold in that dank little room, so I spent the winter vacation in the library hovering close to the Internet in wait for word from him. I staked a computer out for myself on the third floor, and to pass the time between refresh clicks and concerned e-mails from Ma and annoying Arabic chain mail from Baba, I burrowed through the university's stacks. The American University in Cairo's library was one of the best in the Middle East: it gave me access to rare books on pre-Islamic poetry, the Egyptian avant-garde of the 1940s, and the eternally outlawed *Lolita*, which was certainly not available at libraries in Doha or Puyallup. I even found out in the cultural anthropology section that the strange wailing was peasant women hired to theatrically mourn when a person died.

This area of the library was overgrown with outdated anthro-esoterica and had evaded pruning for at least thirty years. After nine months at AUC, I had been dropped into the center of the then very vogue political debate about the future of Arab identity and American foreign policy. Although I might have been both Arab and American, I still felt I had no place in the discussions. While waiting for Su-hail in my granite tower, I cultivated a taste for the Oriental-ist curiosities and out-of-print accounts of "native peoples" that sheltered in the metal racks of Dewey Decimal 301. If my classmates like Magda or Mohamed had known I took pleasure loitering in the politically shady vines of the pre-post-colony, I'd have been pariahed for sure. But in a way I think it was an unintentional punk gesture after months of circular complaint about the disparaging portrayal of Arab men in American films and the offensive attire of Princess Jasmine. I didn't give a fuck anymore about what Edward Said said—I just wanted to look at turn-of-last-century nude photographs of tattooed Ouled Nail tribeswomen.

As far as I was concerned, the fewer the readers who had bothered to come that way before me, the more likely the book was to be interesting. One example of a prize find was a 1941 first-person diarization of a feral child. The book was called *Wolf Child, Human Child: Being a Narrative Interpre-tation of the Life History of Kamala, the Wolf Girl*, and was written by an imaginative pediatrician, Arnold Gesell. He ventriloquized his subject's memoirs with great care to de-tail. He described to dreamy effect the rutty scent of Kama-la's wolf-mother's den. There was a plucky description of her fierce spirit as she learned to run on all fours and a plaintive passage about how she so wished to howl at the moon like the other cubs in her pack. How Kamala had managed to dictate her life story to Gesell was never touched on in the book. The pictures of Kamala and her little sister, Amala, were amazing and sad. They stared up at the camera un-comprehendingly, with shredded chicken feathers dusting

THE GIRL WHO FELL TO EARTH

the ground of their new home in the yard of a nunnery. They looked miserable and out of place, but I doubt they would have looked any more healthy had a photo been taken of them in the den.

The library closed at 8 p.m. every night. It was a time I'd dread, as I had to go back out into the streets, hail a cab, and get back to the boat. I'd get back and sit up with my phone on the balcony overlooking the garden on the bank and prepare to spend my evening dialing and redialing with a supply of international phone cards, trying to get through to Suhail, who just never seemed to be in his apartment.

Sometimes I'd get so lonely I actually resorted to calling my parents. Baba was always in a *majlis* somewhere full of loud men. He pressured me to pray and start wearing *hijab*. He had never been pushy before, but he told me about a new sheikh who had come to town and was helping him get back to the "original" Islam. I evaded answering his questions about the particulars of my living situation, and when I brought up the possibility of going to New York City he always offered the same chant of discouragement, "Qatar is your home. Your family are here. This is where you belong." I knew the only reason he said this was because he was more afraid of New York than he was of Cairo. Sure, in comparison to the Gulf it was dangerous and dirty, but that's what I wanted.

Ma, on the other hand, didn't want to hear anything about Egypt or my living situation. Instead she wanted to talk about September 11. "Honey, you don't know what nine-one-one was like here," she said, voice almost cracking with the media-stirred emotion. Where once the glittering green of air raids over Baghdad had filled her with undue anxiety for Baba, now she was howling in the light of the rocket's red glare. I could follow the changing lexicon and vocabulary of U.S. television news in our increasingly strained conversations. How unlike my independent-thinking, hypercritical mother this was. At some point I stopped calling them. I was as alienated from my mother's newfound patriotism as I was from my father's new conservative streak. But if these conversations threw the distance between my mother, father, and me into sharp relief, the lack of communication with Suhail made me feel even further adrift.

It was on an evening in the spring as I sat out trying to call Suhail that a person I'd never seen before stepped into the gate off the street. Judging by the Vans on his feet and the serious headphones haloing his head, I guessed he was an American. His arms were covered with scars and branding, and the tip of a large tattoo peeked out of the neck of his shirt. Despite all the attention-grabbing body modification, his eyes were the most striking thing about him. They flickered back and forth without ever looking away. When they settled on me, feet up on the rail, scratched out phone cards scattered around me like fallen leaves, I had the feeling he was rapid-scanning everything about me. The wailing started again up the river a ways, a haunting noise rising from behind the black silhouette of palm trees.

His name was Si, and as I had guessed, he was from America, a little town called Cloudcroft, New Mexico. Like many young people disenchanted with America after September 11, Si was a recent convert to Islam. Friendship was immediate and easy between us, the kind that might only happen when two unlikely people meet way off their usual courses.

He had moved in upstairs with the Egyptian boys and was in Cairo to learn Arabic so he could read Quran.

As the months wore on, I spent more and more time avoiding my own tomb-like cabin full of unsent letters to Suhail and unspent phone cards by hiding out in Si's room upstairs. He was an amazing distraction, full of gripping anecdotes about the bums, cage fighters, and rural radio DJs he had grown up with. He reminded me a lot of Joey and came from the same world of squats and railroading before he'd gone straight-edge and then Muslim. I pried from him every detail of his three-year journey hitching his way up the West Coast to Alaska while he bused tables at greasy spoons and diners. He regaled me with stories of his old girl-friends: shaved-headed hippie chicks, bottle-blond cougars, L.A. punkettes, and Detroit strippers. It sounded like a cata-logue, but every woman on his list had her own love story, an elaborate drama that I listened to in awe. The concept of falling in love more than once was liberating. The idea that my identity might not be yoked up to my tribe or my father or my first love made me secretly crow with the possibilities. Maybe I didn't have to be so faithful and obsessive about the ever-receding Suhail. I remembered Ma's long, lonely days in Apartment 1303, and how contagious her sadness had been. In all likelihood, I decided, Suhail had forgotten about me; now was the time to give him, or at least the idea of him, up. This is when Suhail waned further and further from me as Si and all his stories waxed brightly in the foreground.

In all the months I'd spent up at Si's apartment, hanging out in mine had ended up becoming an unspoken taboo. I felt hotly self-conscious when we finally lay together on

my bed one evening watching the river run past the open
windows. We'd had dinner together and I'd spilled all the
lingering confusion about Suhail out in one tearful sitting.

"I'm *tired* of waiting," I complained, hearing uncomfortable echoes of Ma's voice in my own. "It's like he's this refrigerator hum in my mind. Always there."

I moaned at Si and flopped down on the bed like a plank.
"What if he never even comes back?"

Si lay down beside me and stroked my hair. "Just go to
sleep. You'll feel better in the morning."

But I didn't feel any better in the morning, I woke from
a nightmare of drowning, gasping in the early morning light
that spilled through the shutter slats. I looked over at Si,
cheek smooshed against the pillow, snoring lightly. I wanted
to be free of everyone's expectations, including my own. In
that angry moment all I wanted was to get on with my life
and to stop living in this limbo Suhail had perhaps unwit-
tingly plunged me into. With that thought, I did something I
never would have expected. Removing my clothes, I crawled
back into bed with Si and I hugged him. Si smiled in his
sleep and stretched. He reached his hand out to my belly
and woke when he felt me naked. His expression shifted
from surprise to confusion to fear back to surprise, and before he could say anything, I planted a klutzy kiss on him.

The last thing you want to think about when you're losing
your virginity is your parents. But I suspect more often than
not, we do imagine their judgment at that moment. I had to
remind myself repeatedly that this choice had nothing to do
with anybody but me. I knew that even if Suhail did come
to Cairo, he would inevitably leave me again. To strip this

rite of passage of its emotional tumult would mean that I was free. I bled a small, oblong heart shape onto the sheet. Afterward, Si took me to the bathroom and washed me off carefully with a rag. We sat in silence for a while listening to the nasal muezzin calling Kit Kat to prayer, and Si put his cheek on my knee and said, "Thank you."

We slept for a while, until my phone rang. I jolted out of my little bed and patted around the floor for my Nokia. I was more shocked than happy to hear Suhail's voice on the other end.

"Where have you *been*? I've been trying to get through to you all night!" He sounded frantic and worried. "I'm coming to Cairo to see you next week! I routed through on my way back to Doha. I can only stay one night. I miss you!"

I barely breathed while listening to Suhail's excited voice while I worked out what the correct response to this news might be. "Miss you too," I answered limply, and clicked off my phone. Si left without saying a word; he understood. My little boat cabin had become my bubble, the tin can I floated in, disturbed only at night by the boys above and in the morning by the fisherman along the side. I wasn't sure I was ready to open it up yet, but now I would be forced to. Suhail expected that all would be as it always was, that my feelings would remain unchanged and true. But the situation had changed from under him in his absence and the fact was that Suhail had become a subplot.

That week I cleaned the flat, scrubbed the sheet, and generally disinfected the rooms, erasing the past six months of occupancy for Suhail's arrival. When I'd finished, it was pleasantly anonymous. It could have been anywhere, any time, minus the mighty river flowing outside. I set a plan to make good on my promise to Suhail. I had read about a similar dilemma in a story about a village girl in Upper Egypt and decided it would be better to give him my virginity as a symbolic gesture rather than tell him the truth. I filled the fridge with fresh food for the first time and went to the butcher, where I bought lamb and filled a courtesy jam jar with fresh blood. I had no idea if this scheme was going to work outside a literary context.

The next Thursday Suhail appeared at the street gate in an oversized leather bomber jacket. Hanafi was dubious and came down to double-check with me before letting him in. He did look kind of shifty not wearing a *thobe*. He gave Hanafi an absurd tip; still, Hanafi didn't seem impressed with this *Khaleeji* on his turf.

"Alone together at last," Suhail said when we were locked into my little room. His tone was light and breezy and his accent sounded American, not Qatari. "So are you still planning on coming to New York next year?"

I'd forgotten all about my plans for NYU. That application was *never* going to get sent. New York seemed like such a long way away. Slowly it dawned on me that Suhail really didn't think anything was different. What had I done? My voice came out blunt and loud. "I don't know where I'll be next year, or any year." This surprised him. "Who knows when we'll see each other again?"

He said the right thing: "I'll wait as long as it takes."

I said the wrong thing: "I won't."

His happiness to see me was difficult to reconcile with the year of silence. Now, for the first time with no authority

THE GIRL WHO FELL TO EARTH

figures, no uncles or teachers or compound guards between us, we could barely touch each other. He'd flown halfway around the world to take my virginity, and I'd two-timed him. It was unbearable. I borrowed a pipe from upstairs and fixed him up a grape *shisha* on the deck. While he sat outside, I ladled the blood with a teaspoon into a whisper-thin plastic baggie and deposited it beside the bed. I felt sick. It was a hot evening, and I went back out to the rail to gulp a few deep breaths out of the musty river air. Some shirtless kids were jumping off the railway bridge upstream into the river. "Idiots," Suhail coughed in Arabic after a long gurgle from the pipe. Their screams as they plummeted into the murky water echoed off the banks, and I felt dread welling up ready to bring me to my knees like acrophobia. At that moment I'd have happily jumped in with the "idiots" to avoid seeing my stupid plan through. Somewhere on the balcony above I could hear the bubble of Si's *shisha* pipe and saw the reflection of a light from his room, a yellow streak in the greasy gray water. I thought of climbing the ladder to talk this through with him but knew I'd never go up there again.

When I'd finally gotten a handle on myself, I put Suhail's pipe away and took him to the bedroom. I changed into a white *jalabiya* that I hoped would evoke a certain rustic innocence. Outside, the river surged past, silent and dangerous, and although we stayed in one place, everything changed around us.

When I closed my eyes, I couldn't see Suhail and I couldn't picture what Si looked like. Mercifully, my parents made no cameo appearance this time. I was floating in empty space and shifted to autopilot. I had imagined this moment so many times, of how I'd be positively effervescent with emotion, but instead all I felt was a deep, dull emptiness. I didn't dare move for fear I'd bust my bag of blood before it was time, and lay there trying to cup it in the small of my back. I hovered imperceptibly over the sheet while Suhail figured things out. I winced when he pushed in. I delivered my line, "Ouch." He hitched up my legs to see the blood. I struggled to frame the stain in a more convincing spot, knocking skulls with him as we both looked down at the result.

Suhail went to the bathroom to get a damp towel and returned, patting me down clinically. I lay back, rubbing the blood off my back and onto the sheet. This time it was more a bloody shadow than an oblong heart. He also lay back down and put his head on my belly. "I'm sorry," he said, and within seconds had taken off dreaming as I listened to the scuttling under the floorboards.

The next afternoon I accompanied Suhail to the airport, where we hugged awkwardly to an audience of very prying eyes.

"I'll see you in Doha next *Eid*?"

"Sure," I told him, though I knew it wasn't going to happen.

As soon as I got into the cab, a heavy blanket of exhaustion fell over me. In contrast to the first time I'd ridden into Cairo from the airport, it seemed as if the city were on mute, air sticky with a charge like that before a storm. When I made it back to Kit Kat, I slammed the gate on its iron hinges. Hanafi was sitting on a lawn chair enjoying a quiet night in the garden. As I took the stairs three steps at a time, he yelled, "Little by little!" warning me to slow down. The force of my flight ended with my hips pitted against the rail of my deck. I had a scream scraping up my insides but couldn't let it out. I needed to do something to get out of and get over myself. I scrambled up the ladder past Si's room and up onto the roof. From there I could see much farther out along the flat tops of the other boats, downriver to Agouza and upriver to Imbaba.

I heard the mourner ladies' voices wailing somewhere along the banks beyond my view. I tried to scream, but it just came out in a wheezy, crippled whine. Like Kamala, I was a yippy, feral child faking her way into being a wolf. I would never have the right vocal cords to muster a real howl. That was part of being an alien—I'd never be so deeply rooted as to feel the most profound pain. I realized in a bewildered flush that I had no reason to mourn the skin I'd just shed. Could I really be so ungrateful as to forget the fact that I was free? I could say what I wanted and even see whom I wanted; now I had nothing to prove. I looked down into the swirling river, blacker than the Puyallup river and far wider. From here it felt like being on the edge of a cliff. I was terrified and exhilarated, and didn't think I could trust myself not to jump. The water was flowing north, I calculated. If those kids on the bridge could jump into the middle of the river, I could certainly make the jump from here. Hadn't I been thrown into the deep end as a baby? I'd throw myself into the Nile. A rebirth. According to my calculations, the current would just carry me over to the bank, and I'd wash up in the bulrushes and pull myself out, *easy*. I backed up a few steps on the roof of the boys' apartment, practiced my pacing once, and then, before I could stop myself, I jumped, only remembering Ma's advice from the swimming pool to tuck my head in on a dive *after* I'd crashed into the Nile with a graceless belly flop.

Every day we pass farther away from the time spent in our mothers' wombs, our mammalian diving reflex grows weaker. When I opened my eyes in the murky river I couldn't tell which way was up. With the water lit only dimly by the lights on the boat, panic rather than instinct set in as I bobbed up, thrashing for breath, and went under again. I realized dimly that I'd miscalculated. The flow in the middle of the river was north, but the edges close to the banks formed an undertow, and now I was being dragged under the pilings of the boat by a stealth current. My baggy clothes were pulling me down, heavy like lead. I ended up under the house in the pitch-black filth. I felt the surprisingly big bodies of fish curl and brush my legs in the dark. I gasped at the brief pockets of air that came with the bobbing of the boat and went under again, now calling back to the rescue those lessons spent practicing the dead man's float with Dima and Ma in the Apartment 1303 pool in Doha.

When I opened my eyes again, it was like in a dream, and time really did slow, just like they say it does in an accident. My heart sounded distant to me, like a Joe Meek track's satellite-echo in space, and I knew absolutely for the first time why my mother had always wanted me to swim. A flash of light broke the murk, and I yelped under the water for help. Another gasp of air came, and I gave up fighting, letting the current pull me all the way under the boat and out the other side, where Hanafi fished me out by my armpits. I was so dazed from the jump I didn't care and couldn't really hear what he was yelling at me. I knew I had to take a shower immediately before I got bilharzia, and then I should vomit up any water I'd swallowed. Despite all of this I felt a bizarre elation, a powerful feeling of control after having lost control.

21

DELTA GEMINORUM •
MIDDLE OF THE SKY • وسط السماء

After my stunt jumping off the boat, I received a call from
the landlady.

"We agreed you'd keep a low profile," she said coldly. "Instead, you've drawn a lot of attention to yourself."

I knew but didn't want to acknowledge what she was in-
ferring.

"You understand my concerns." There was a spiny suggestion in her tone that made me rise to her bait.

"I'm leaving anyway," I replied.

I returned to spending most of my time in the sanctuary
of the library and surfed couches in Agouza, Zamalek, Garden City, and Mounira. Thankfully the library was still open
all through the summer. With no coursework or required
readings or in-box to hover over, I drifted back to the 301s.
It was while hunting for something called *Space-Time of the
Bororo of Brazil* that a small book caught my eye. I pried it
out of the tight shelf to read the spine: *Born Under a Wander-
ing Star* by Dr. Harold Stark. This was stamped in crooked
silver embossing, and like many of the library's acquisitions
from the 1980s, it had been rebound by the university in an

appealingly mysterious tar-black leather. Most things about it were unremarkable. As with everything else in this corner of the library, the book was written by a white male, was an account of his travels with an untamed people, and was full of fulsome observations and eulogies for a way of life that had no hope of resisting modernity. There was nothing to signify how precious it might actually be to me.

That is, until I came to the subtitle, which leaped out at me and made my heart race: *Night Journeys of the Al-Dafira Bedouin.* I let out a little yelp of surprise. The book was dedicated "To all the youth of the Al-Dafira, who face probably the greatest changes of any people in the world." I let out more little yelps of disbelief and excitement as I leafed through the pages. The book was full of pictures. Photos of a town, of trackers and their sons, pictures of male faces I recognized in my own. There were diagrams of living arrangements that matched up with our tents in Saudi, drawings of Umi Safya's tripod for milk churning, and detailed drawings of her weaving designs. All these little details I had observed myself were now retold to me as anthropology. It was too weird. There was even an explanation of the tic-tac-toe-style game we used to play in the sand with the white rocks and dry black goat turds. At first I felt indignant. How did this guy know all this?

But I was also breathless from this discovery. I had one more surprise in store. On the last page of the book was a black-and-white photo of the young anthropologist Harold Stark, dressed in full Al-Dafira regalia, complete with baldric holster, Omani-style dagger, and *gutra*. The description was brief. There were a few mentions of his areas of expertise, including his work studying the poetry of Sinai tribes and the astronomy of the Bedouin in the Negev. The last line in the book read, "Stark continues his research in Cairo, where he is a lecturer at the American University."

The book was older than I was, so I didn't expect to find his name in the staff directory. But there it was, complete with contact details. I clicked his name and sent him a frantic-sounding message of introduction. Dr. Stark replied within minutes. I was nervous while I waited in the long white hallway of the anthropology department for him to show up at his office. When he arrived he respectfully *didn't* shake my hand.

"Call me Abdul Hayy. I changed it from Harold a long time ago. Gone native. Your e-mail was a serendipitous surprise for me. A stroke of fate, I think."

Dr. Stark wore a trim white beard, a skullcap, and the short-style *thobe* of a religious man. He listened patiently while I explained the particulars of, well, *everything*—how I'd come to find his book, how I'd come to be in Cairo, and, of course, how I had come into being in the first place. He responded to my gush at having found this treasure trove of information about my family in true academic style: "The life your father led was premodern, elemental; it must seem irreconcilably foreign to a digital native like yourself."

I suddenly felt inadequate and uninteresting. At ten years old I had played *Oregon Trail* on a computer, shooting squirrels with pixel bullets and getting virtual dysentery on a wagon train. My father, at ten, was on an actual epic trek, hunting with an actual falcon and risking very real tuberculosis while riding in a bona fide camel caravan.

Dr. Stark switched into astonishing Al-Dafira dialect and addressed me by my Arabic name. "Safya, I was eager to meet you because I need your help."

A native informant, to use an anthropological term, was what he really needed, but because he couldn't find one who could use a camera and, most importantly, one who was a female, I would perhaps do. He needed someone young and spry who could communicate with the women of the current tribe he was studying, the Qarasin Bedouin in eastern Sinai. Shady as that might sound, it was my ticket out of a listless summer of imposing on other people's hospitality. The job was simple: climb into the mountains with a woman named Kawthar while she herded the goats to graze and record her oral history along the way.

"Try particularly to get stories about her father. He was a famous smuggler and poet who composed beautiful verse from jail," Dr. Stark told me. I had concerns about my level of comprehension but he deflected my concerns. "You'll find it very easy to speak with them. Most Bedu Arabic is astonishingly similar."

Either way, I was nervous. Dr. Stark furnished me with a video camera and paid for a private ride into Sinai. No passports? No problem. We took the back way, passing half-finished hotels and summer lodges that had been abandoned in the mire of bureaucracy and zoning as the Israeli-Egyptian border passed back and forth over the years. I caught glimpses of these ghost homes, Sinai's forgotten dreams just crumbling in the wind.

The Qarasin territory was along the coast and backed up

into the mountains, where hidden plateaus and crags in the rock hid oases, and pastures for the goats to munch. The Qarasin had managed to maintain a reasonably traditional lifestyle despite the unusually intense politics of their turf, which contained Palestinian border tunnels, international smuggling routes, a secretive Israeli security presence, and Egyptian police patrols. Add this volatile mix to the tourist developments built for sunbathing and reef diving—and the fact that a sizable chunk of their land had been colonized by a strange new tribe of dreadlocked German, French, and Israeli people who referred to themselves collectively as "Rainbow"—and it's nothing short of miraculous that the clan had survived at all into this strange time. Compared to Al-Dafira they had far more interaction with the outside world, so the fact that the tribe was still relatively nomadic made them both something of a marvel and extremely sought-after quarry for historians, sociologists, and anthropologists like Dr. Stark.

A road cut through between their base camp and the groves and meadows in their mountains. It carried Israeli hippies to the beaches in the south and Korean pilgrims to Mount Sinai in the interior. When I arrived there it was night. I walked a little way into the water and let the Red Sea baste me. Patches of phosphorescent plankton clustered a little way out in the black water and, for a moment, I couldn't tell if it was stars or the sea. I sculled out to them and floated on my back, spinning myself in a circle, sending ripples out to lap all shores. The water was gentle, the perfect antidote to the swirling confusion that had nearly drowned me in Cairo.

Here, in one of the most symbolically loaded, fought-over plots of land on earth, it was a total paradox that life should suddenly seem so much simpler.

I spent the first week under the wing of Kawthar, a very petite chain-smoking mother of seven who kept me close and let me film her while she went about her days. There was little that was poetic about Kawthar. She was sort of a cross between Ma in personality and Aunt Moody in her dress. The smoking left a little circle of white in the black fabric of her face veil. It sucked into her mouth when she spoke, then reappeared like a punctuating period when she'd ended her sentences. I filmed her—a lot. I stopped only to recharge the batteries with the extensions from a generator. I wasn't sure quite how to broach the subject of folktales or poetic *qasaid* or her famous outlaw father when the day was so full of these "exotic" people doing, well, normal shit. I shot tapes and tapes of Kawthar hand-washing the family's laundry in a bucket (and finding her daughter's red G-string). I filmed her chopping up salad (impressive without a chopping board). I sat by, electrical tape over the little red recording light, while she yelled at her kids for playing chicken with a semitruck, watched must-see TV (a badly dubbed Turkish soap opera everyone was talking about), and strung shiny beads onto thread to sell to the Rainbow Tribe farther down the beach. The only thing that was picturesque in the romantic sense I'd been sent to capture was the epic landscape we were pitched against.

One afternoon I sat with Kawthar while she embroidered a big black wedding shawl with silver sequins, videotaping the light glinting on the long, beautiful pattern. But even then she interrupted the "timeless" shot I knew Dr. Stark wanted me to get by hacking a tubercular-sounding cough and lighting up a cigarette that she left dangling in her mouth, squinting away the smoke like a female Clint Eastwood.

Kawthar's husband was curious about me. He had been the University's contact for this project, and so he often appeared out of nowhere to ask questions, then disappeared again for days. He and most of the other men were rarely around the camp, especially at night, when it was generally understood they were out somewhere up to no good.

"I'm very curious. Where are you from?" He spoke to me in Israeli-accented English rubbed off from years of taxiing people. "You're not Egyptian, are you? You looks Egyptian but something tells me no."

Here was a man used to dealing with tourists on spiritual quests. I tried a friendly mug and shook my head no.

"Indian?" He squinted at me, trying to read the small signs. He answered his own question: "No. I have it, you are Spanish!" His observation had the confident delivery of a wildly guessing fortune-teller. "I suppose it doesn't matter. We are all the same, no?" He pretended to be disinterested, hoping I'd take the bait. But he couldn't resist the guessing game for long. "Moroccan? Tunisian? Turkish? Italian?"

He thought he had me pinned. And maybe he did. I was neither surprised nor pleased with his guesses. "Just give me time," he said, and returned back out to the darkness somewhere down near the beach.

"Don't let on to the men where you're from," Kawthar warned me that night. It had been an uncomfortable encounter. Her husband must have badgered her about my background. "Believe me. It'll just cause trouble if they know your family are Bedu. Better they think you're just a foreigner."

The next morning we headed up into the mountains with a herd of about twenty goats. Almost as soon as we'd passed out of sight of the road and the main camp below, everyone was louder and more boisterous, and the faces came out. Kawthar walked uphill fast with a baby goat on one shoulder and her youngest son on the other, all the while smoking. I felt ill from the hike, and all I had to lug was the camera. When we made our camp in a *wadi* against a ridge the first night, Kawthar introduced me to the others. I set up the camera on its tripod, set up a light near Kawthar, and introduced myself variously as Safya or Sophia, depending on which one tripped out of my mouth first.

While Kawthar prepared a satellite dish for making bread, she asked, "So what's your name really?"

"Whichever."

I pressed *record* to capture Kawthar's incredible repurposing of an old hunk of technology.

"What do you mean, *whichever?*"

"I mean, it's both."

She poured the runny flour and water in a spiral over the hot metal dome, and I came in for a close-up of the bubbling batter. "I don't understand. How do you write it when you sign?" she asked me.

"In English I write Sophia, but in Arabic I write it Safya." I demonstrated with my finger in the sand.

"Bah." She flipped the bread on the satellite dish.

I knew she wasn't interested in all my noncommittal

answers, but I wanted to clarify. Shift the blame off of myself. "In my official documents one says Safya and the other says Sophia."

"Screw official documents!" She jabbed a twig under the metal dome to rustle the embers. Kawthar had had international borders shift across her land from Egypt to Israel and back again, and with each shift there was renewed bureaucracy, renewed bullshit. I should have known she'd be dubious of officialdom.

"*Khelli welli!* See if I care! What's important is your folks. What do they call you?"

I knew she wouldn't be satisfied by this answer, either. "My American family calls me Sophia, and my Bedu family calls me Safya." I was beginning to realize that somewhere along the line (I'm not sure where) the name thing had morphed into a serious psycholinguistic problem.

Kawthar's chin jutted under her veil. "Girl, no wonder you're so confused. Your stars were cast too far apart," she said mysteriously, and flipped the spiral of batter that had now burned into bread.

"Can you do that again?" I asked her to repeat the performance of bread-making for the camera, and this time I made sure to shut up.

The next morning we set out for higher ground, farther up in the mountains. Kawthar wanted to check on some date palms her husband had laid claim to the year before. A few of us took a detour up into a thin crack in the rock while the drove of goats stayed down below. We climbed up and up the sandy gravel into a little valley surrounded on all sides by steep rock walls. The vegetation was so thick we had to wrestle through the boughs and tall grass. I wondered how many other pockets like this there were in the barren cliffs we had wandered through. It would be invisible from anywhere but above.

"How do you find places like this?" I asked, in awe of the secret oasis that had appeared from the middle of what looked like barren rock.

"By fate," Kawthar replied with conviction. She had already hacked her way through the tall grass to the far end of the little valley. "Someone's been here!" she yelled back to the rest of us.

We broke a path down to the water and looked across to where Kawthar stood at the stump of a fallen palm. It and several of the largest trees had been burned down and had collapsed into the pool. Their ash filled the water that had collected there, the charred-black trunks flaking away.

That night around the fire the ladies got to talking. Someone had picked up a radio show from Saudi briefly on her portable radio. It was a call-in show during which you could anonymously ask a venerable Muslim scholar about your deepest concerns. As soon as we'd quieted down, a woman's voice came on and asked the cleric a very deep question indeed. "What should I do if my husband wants anal sex?"

A roar of laughter went up around the group of women; some of the goats spooked at the cackles as they echoed around the canyon. Marwa, Kawthar's fourteen-year-old daughter—the one whose red G-string we had discovered a few days before—was confused about the terminology.

"What are they talking about? What's that mean?" she whined to her mother and aunts, but none of them bothered explaining to her, as they were too wrapped up in opening their own conversation about their men.

The banter was becoming very raunchy when, without solicitation, they turned to me. I froze in the headlights as they hassled me to fess up about the men in my life. Before I had the presence of mind to turn the camera off, I was giving them the dish about the double whammy of Si and Suhail. I hadn't spoken to anyone about it yet and so I told them everything, about the sneaking around in Doha, about the waiting around in Cairo, about the blood from the butcher's, and even about jumping into the river. I swallowed the choke that rose in my throat with the thought of either boy. By the time my cathartic confession was over, I'd worked myself up into fat tears that felt greasy mixed with the layer of sand on my cheeks. I fully expected a stern silence and perhaps a long walk back alone, but Kawthar and the women surprised me. If they were appalled or scandalized, this last bastion of true, traditional Bedu life didn't show it. Instead, they laughed at me. Some were so hysterical they had to walk away to catch their breath.

"Who do you think you are, Qais and Laila?" Kawthar scoffed, referencing the tragic characters of Arabic poetry's own *Romeo and Juliet*. "Jumping off the boat? What is this, a *film Hindi*?"

I tried hard to screw up a smile that would hide the sheepish, stunned look frozen on my face.

"Anyway, the real question is what's the white guy's *thing* look like?"

That evening I was comforted by hearing the various stories of their wedding nights. Marwa and I listened, silent and dopy as kids eavesdropping on grown-up talk at the dinner table. The women all took turns describing their nuptials, whether they'd gone to bed willingly or not.

"I was so scared that night, these two rolled me up in a blanket and threw me into my new husband's tent," Kawthar spat while her sisters-in-law rolled around laughing.

"It was like feeding a chunk of meat to a lion!" one of them snapped back at Kawthar between wheezy little hoots.

Kawthar delivered her comeback deadpan: "Why didn't you take me to a *real* lion, huh? Should have taken me to a different tent." There was a twinkle in her eye as she stroked her daughter's hair. "Anyway, that night is always just the beginning," Kawthar added, and winked at me from across the fire.

With that wink, I felt absolved. My fears of having fucked up irreversibly then began to erode with each wave of confession.

We spent another week in the mountains grazing the goats. The last night, Kawthar agreed to recite some of her father, Anez Abu Salim's, poetry from his time in prison. She began,

"The world endures, the sky moves by plan,
Fate's rope ensnares us wherever it can."

My heart sank. I'd used my tapes up. Kawthar saw I was upset about something and stopped. "Let it go," she consoled me as I rifled through the camera bag for a tape I could record over. "*Ya* what's-your-name, some things are not meant to be kept. Forget it."

Still crestfallen at my failure to record anything useful, I left the next afternoon. Kawthar's husband gave me a ride to where the night bus to Cairo would pick me up. He was blasting Mohammed Abdu out the rolled-down windows of his truck, the same make as Faraj's in Doha but with wood slats fencing the back to hold in all the goats. He dropped me off at the unmarked bus stop and grinned out the open door at me.

"I figured it out."

"What?"

"Where you're from."

I sat down on a big rock and squinted back into the truck at him. "Go ahead." I nodded.

"We've agreed you're not Turkish or Israeli or Spanish. You're not an Arab. You're not an American. The way I see it, you must be an alien!" he declared with a cheeky grin.

Why disappoint him? "Yes. That's it."

He seemed bizarrely satisfied with himself, and I wondered if the joke I'd assumed he'd just made was intentional.

"Safe journey." He raised his hand in the air for a few seconds as he passed and honked twice, two universal signals of acknowledgment, whether between islanders passing on rafts or great cargo ships passing in the night. I was still sitting on the boulder when he disappeared back up the seaside highway in the direction from which we'd come.

With almost an hour before the bus was due, I stuck a tape into the camera to have a look. For most people, hearing your own voice on tape is like fingernails on a blackboard. But hearing my voice over this tape was *bad*. Every single tape of Kawthar and the others was ruined with my babbling voice-over. I hadn't realized how much talking about myself I had done to the poor woman who was supposed to be the subject of these tapes. My narcissism was repulsive to me in hindsight, and Kawthar had systematically turned my questions to her into a question about me. Somehow, I had ended up being the anthropological subject. She reminded me of David Bowie being playful, flipping an interview around on reporters with monosyllabic answers. "No." "Yes." "Sometimes." "Oh. Average." She grilled me about things I never thought about, deflecting every one of my timid inquiries about her stories and songs.

"So you went to Qatar. What were you looking for?"

A crippling cringe gripped me as my voice answered, "I guess I wanted to find myself."

It was just too embarrassing. Worst of all, there was my entire confession about Si and Suhail and all the private talk that came afterward. I couldn't give these tapes to Dr. Stark. Kawthar was right. Some things really weren't meant to be kept. I stacked them out in the road for the next truck to run over and planned what I was going to use as my excuse.

Somewhere about dusk it started to dawn on me that the bus to Cairo was probably not coming. In a panic, I tried hailing the next lights I saw. It took a few tries before a big tourist bus with rearview mirrors jutting out like antennae stopped.

"Where are you going?" the driver asked.

"Cairo."

"We're stopping for the night at Jabal Musa, then on to Cairo."

I wavered for a few seconds, considering trekking back to Kawthar.

"Well? You want on?" the driver asked impatiently. "It's this or sleeping out here. We're the last bus to Cairo tonight."

Convinced, I stepped up into the bus, paid him, and then collapsed into a window seat, taking my place alongside all the drowsy, sunburned tourists. The bus waved in long, smooth turns up into the mountains. The rocking motion put me to sleep, and I fell fast into dreams after weeks of fitful sleep on the rocky ground.

We reached our destination around midnight; a sign marked it out in Arabic, English, Hebrew, and at least ten other languages. Mount Sinai was a formidable-looking peak in the moonlight as it rose up from Saint Catherine's Monastery, a cluster of ancient stone buildings set off bizarrely by the surrounding acreage of pristine, freshly paved parking lot. A crowd of guides swarmed the exit, so I waited for the other passengers to get off before I made my way out into the aisle.

"Where is the bathroom?" I asked the bus driver; he pointed toward Saint Catherine's.

The monastery was already full of people when I crossed the vast parking lot full of buses. I followed signs down one of the corridors to where a group of Midwesterners had gathered around a freakishly large, unhealthy-looking desert shrub growing from a crack in one of the walls. A plaque beside it read "I AM THAT I AM" in ostentatious Copperplate Bold.

"They expect us to believe *that* is the burning bush?" one of the tourists asked in my general direction.

"That's what it says." I shrugged and squeezed past her to get to the toilets.

The lady snorted disapprovingly and turned to pluck a few leaves off as souvenirs.

On my way back across the parking lot, I looked up at the shadowy mountain behind me. A luminous spiral made up of hundreds of lanterns, flashlights, and mobile phones lit an LCD/LED route all the way up the mountain. The spectacle was like a shiny lure to a fish; I decided to follow. Despite the moon being almost full, the trek up the mountain was dark. The path began wide and gentle enough for several people to ride on camelback, but halfway up it dwindled into a thin and gravelly path instead of the majestic ascent most were prepared for. At this point the way turned into a manic zig-zag to the top of the mountain's treeless lip. I passed many types of mountaineer as we pecked our way up through the darkness toward sunrise. There were German students, Fili-pino nuns, and all manner of people making this pilgrimage. All for their own health, historical, or spiritual reasons.

I was one of the first to summit, after a Japanese man with a typical khaki vest full of camera lenses. We had the little plateau at the top to ourselves for a few minutes, and I watched him while he framed up a time-lapse photo of the night sky. Not wanting to interfere with the shot, I found a place hidden a few meters away looking down into a deep valley. First I sat facing east to see the sunrise, then west to catch the stars for a while longer. Even in the desert in my childhood, or the night the tribesman had watched over us, I'd never seen the stars quite so close or the Milky Way so heavily laden.

First, all I noticed was a blinking light, a wink, a streak. Shooting star was my first guess. But it didn't disappear like a piece of space junk fleeting through the sky; it stayed steady on its track. I relaxed my eyes and then I saw it flicker at me brightly. The photographer cursed under his breath about the satellite. A glowing scratch torn through the middle of his carefully framed heaven had ruined his photograph."Racka fracka flipar rip." It sounded like Yosemite Sam's nonsense cussing.

From here it was just a sweet pink flash against the bluing sky, but if it *was* a satellite it was probably broadcasting *Star Trek* episodes and terrorist threats and the rerun voices of old stars like Samira Tawfiq live to millions of color TV sets in the region. I watched it as it passed subtly from one end of the constellation to the other. The Japanese man was now huffing in annoyance as he tried to fend off an Indian family who had brought up our rear and was now strolling cluelessly in front of his tripod. The silence we had been enveloped in for those first few minutes was now broken by a large group of Nigerians bursting into tongues at the door of the little church, and by the Americans from the burning bush loudly exclaiming, "Well, would you look at that!" at the view.

I caught a glance of the moving light again at the corner of my eye and turned back to it. Somehow each individual prick of yellow, orange, and white seemed to be moving on its own, and therefore I concluded *aliens*. Even if it was a man-made object, puny and pathetic beside the great fixed stars, the colors of the lights on it were very impressive. It reminded me of looking into the sky and seeing the stealth bomber for the first time. Then I recognized that this thing was much closer than a satellite and much more complicated than any military craft I'd ever seen from the air base in Puyallup. Its movements were not on any set course and the lights were strange, illusive; it was almost as if I couldn't look at them head-on but had to look in my periphery. I sat there hugging my knees to my chest, not wanting anyone else to see what I saw as I cast my eyes out at these strange lights now swinging over the valley.

That old, nameless urge rose into an ache in my chest. It was an almost hysterical desire to be beamed up with the passing lights, to disappear like some crazed Heaven's Gate fanatic. I grasped for a view of myself, trying hard to get the scheme of things. What I needed most now was to reach escape velocity from myself. I'd already left the orbits of Ma and Baba before I felt the effects of their gravity, of their influence. In fact, neither of their worldviews made sense to me at all; they were just a couple of grand delusions in a universe of chaos and pure chance. Neither Ma's pragmatic ideals of manifest destiny nor Baba's deep belief in the precision of Allah's intention offered any comfort as I sat there quivering on the mount in the middle of my identity crisis. I had been shaped by these opposing polar forces, but I wasn't governed by them anymore, and it took climbing a holy mountain I'd never planned to summit before I could understand that.

My longing to ride up with the lights dissipated as the orbs seemed to dislocate from the craft and fly off, radiating different colors in all directions. A few others saw them but seemed less impressed; intakes of awed breath rippled briefly across the crowd before they turned back to the main event: sunrise. As it rose, the sun dissolved the shadows from the cliffs and trenches all around us. When the others began their descent, I stayed behind a little while. I felt dizzy, hoping deliriously for another display of lights.

That was when I grabbed at the earth to catch myself, like waking from a falling dream. I didn't care anymore where I came from or where I was going; all I wanted was to be on my way. After all, the universe, this planet, my two homelands, and even I would come undone. From politics to particles, everything that made me in every most profound sense was on a constant, polarizing drift, stretching farther and farther apart.

What were the odds? I asked myself, and remembered the long night spent in the desert when we were so small. I stayed on a few more minutes, watching in case the unidentified flying object might signal me again from the setting night sky. But when no more came, I got the message. The possibilities of this life were simply too rare and precious to spend another moment or a million light-years floating around weightless and wayward in the wait. I pulled myself up and, taking giant leaps, made my way down the small steps off the mountain.

ACKNOWLEDGMENTS

Love to my mother and father and sister and siblings and family and tribe for being the rich and loving quarry from which this book was mined.

I owe the existence of this book in particular to these three people:

Michael Vazquez, Shumon Basar, and Peter Webber.

Thanks to *Bidoun* magazine for the years they helped me try out and refine ideas, Deena Chalabi for being a second brain when I needed one, and Wassan Al-Khudhairi for all her support.

Thank you to my agents, Kevin Conroy Scott and Sophie Lambert, who offered advice and space and fought for more time whenever it was needed. Also, to my surrogate Gulfie Qabila, who are a constant inspiration: Amal Khalaf, Fatima Al-Qadiri, Hamida Al-Kuwari, Talal Obeid, Manal Al-Dowayan, Rana Jubara, Khalid Al-Gharaballi, Fatima Al-Mostafawi, Sheyma Buali, Mohamed Al-Ibrahim, the Al-Humaidi sisters, Aziz Al-Qatemi and Abdulla Al-Misnad.

Thanks to Chris Kyung for the beautiful map. Love to the Sulkosky fort and the Carmichael base. A big thank-you to everyone who read, gave notes, edited, or listened to me moan, from the earliest scraps of the proposal to the final drafts: Jaime Tung, Malak Helmy, Ben Robinson, Marika Lyandysu, Alexander Provan, Simeon Roos-Evstes, Anand Balakrishnan, Philip Chaffee, and Lena Tutanjian. A major debt is owed to Her Excellency Sheikha Al Mayassa Al Thani for making many of my abandoned dreams come true quite by chance.

And finally, to Sensei for keeping his Secret so well.

GLOSSARY

Abaya—A long cloak-like dress worn by women in the Arabian Gulf. Sartorial cousins to the floor-skimming garments of Batman, Darth Vader, and Neo.

Accesswarat—English-Arabic pidgin for barrettes, hair ribbons, and other accessories.

Ajera—A large club with a knob on the end for clobbering (see Fred Flintstone).

Asha—Dinner (also refers to evening prayer).

Athan—The call to prayer.

Berga—Bedouin face veil with a vertical thread hung between the eyes; not to be confused with the burkas of Afghanistan.

Bowab—Doorman to residential buildings in Egypt; equivalent to a super in a New York City apartment.

Burra!—Get out! Scram!

Djinn—A genie closer in look and character to a gremlin than to Robin Williams.

Dukkan—Bodega, corner shop, minimart, superette.

Fajer—Dawn (also refers to morning prayer).

Fatiha—The opening verse of the Quran.

Film Hindi—When a minor drama spirals into a major show of emotional pyrotechnics.

Garumba—An affectionate name for a dilapidated car. English synonyms: beater, jalopy, rattletrap.

Gutra—Male headdress.

Halal—Permissible foodstuff or activity.

Halawa—Body wax often prepared in the home. Ingredients vary from country to country; however, almost all recipes consist of sugar, lemon juice, and a liberal dose of de Sade.

Hawli—Get down/out/off!

Hijab—Your common garden-variety veil.

Imam—leader of prayer in a mosque.

Jalabiya—Loose-fitting indoor dress of women in the Gulf, not to be confused with the Egyptian galabiya; similar in function to a muumuu.

Kaaba—The black cuboid building Muslims pray toward.

Kepsa—Fine Bedouin cuisine.

Khalas—Enough!

Khaleeji—Adjective to describe something of or from the Arabian Gulf.

Khayal—Shadows/imaginings.

Kuss umak ahmar—Mighty swear meaning "Your mother's cunt is red."

Maghreb—Dusk (also refers to sunset prayer).

Majlis—Men's parlor.

Masha'Allah—God made it so (used to express awe or to rebut a compliment to avoid accidentally giving something the evil eye).

Mashrabia—Carved woodwork usually placed over a window; historically used to allow women to look out of the harem but no one to look in.

Mawwāl—Arabic song introduction during which the vocalist pronounces vowels for longer than usual.

Moda—The fashion. If something is *Al-Moda* it's in style.

Niqab—A common type of face veil.

Oud—Sandalwood.

Qasida (s.) / Qasaid (pl.)—Traditional Arabic ode in tripartite structure.

Rakat—Units of prayer.

Shaabi—Adjective meaning "folk," or sometimes "street."

Shadafa—Bidet-like spray hose found in most Middle Eastern toilets.

Shahada—The Muslim declaration of witness that there is no God but God and Mohamed is his prophet.

Shala—Long black scarf worn by women in the Gulf to cover their hair and *boofs*.

Shaytan—Devil.

Saksuka—Goatee.

Simsar—Egyptian slang for real-estate agent.

Sirwal—Underwear.

Souq—Marketplace.

Thobe—Men's long white dress worn in the Gulf region.

Ya ain ya layl—A common Arabic phrase used to introduce a poetic narrative and in music to provide the base from which to improvise the entrance into a song.

Yalla—Come on! A phrase commonly shouted by extras in Hollywood films depicting Arabic-speaking rabble.

Yawm Al-Qiyamah—Judgment Day.

SOPHIA AL-MARIA is an artist, writer, and film-maker. She studied comparative literature at the American University in Cairo, and aural and visual cultures at Goldsmiths, University of London. Her work has been exhibited at the Sharjah biennale, Art Dubai, the New Museum in New York, and the Architectural Association in London. Her writing has appeared in *Harper's*, *Five Dials*, *Triple Canopy*, and *Bidoun*. She works at Mathaf: Arab Museum of Modern Art in Qatar, where she researches Gulf futurism.